THE YOGA-DARSANA

THE YOGA-DARSANA

THE SUTRAS OF PATANJALI WITH THE BHASYA OF VYASA

TRANSLATED INTO ENGLISH

WITH NOTES

From Vachaspati Misras Tattvavaisaradi, Vijnana Bhiksu's Yogavartika and Bhoja's Rajamartanda

By

GANGANATHA JHA

GYAN

Published by

Gyan Publishing House
5, Ansari Road
Daryaganj, New Delhi-110002
Phone: 011-47034999, 9811692060
E-mail: books@gyanbooks.com

Distribution Network
gyanbooks.com
India, USA, Canada, UK, Australia, France

ISBN : 978-81-212-9781-3 (PB)
First Published, 1907

2nd Impression 2023

Printed at: Gyan Press, Delhi.

THE YOGA-DARSANA
Author: GANGANATHA JHA

THE
YOGA-DARŚANA.

THE SUTRAS OF PATAÑJALI WITH THE BHĀṢYA OF VYĀSA

TRANSLATED INTO ENGLISH

WITH NOTES

From Vâchaspati Miśrás Tattvavaiśâradî, Vijnána Bhiksu's Yogavârtika and Bhoja's Râjamârtaṇḍa

BY

GANGÂNÂTHA JHÂ,

Professor of Sanskrit, Muir Central College, Allahabad.

1907.

PREFACE.

The translation now placed before the public was prepared so long ago as 1895; and the vicissituides through which the manuscript has passed has made it absolutely impossible for it to undergo any revision. So what is presented here is the work of a mere neophyte in the mysteries of Sanskrit Philosophical translation; and the translator would therefore, at the very outset, offer his apologies to the reader, for his providing for him what he himself considers a rather poor fare. It may however be added, as an extenuating circumstance, that the printing of the old 'copy' was allowed to be continued in view of the undertaking given to the late Mr. Tukaram Tatya—an undertaking from which the translator could not free himself.

The chief fault of the present translation lies in the fact that it is not readable by itself. This has been due to the extremely obscure character of the original, a character which is inseparable from all works dealing with subjects, the whole truth with regard to which cannot be given out to the 'public.' Imperfect as it is, it is expected that it may help, to a slight extent, future workers in the same field.

By way of atoning for this deficiency of the translation, it is proposed to give here a readable *resume* of the teachings of the Yogasutras.

'Yoga' has been defined as the 'nirodha' of the 'vṛitti' of the 'chitta' brought about by 'Practice' and 'Freedom from Attachment'; and the only explanation that will make this intelligible to the ordinary reader is that *yoga* consists in the controlling of the mind;—though it must be admitted that the definition in this form becomes philosophically inaccurate;

as the 'chitta' of the original is something different from 'mind', and 'nirodha', by which is meant 'withdrawal' or 'inhibition' different from 'control.' But all the accurate, renderings of the definition that have been attempted in English have only helped to make the original less intelligible. This 'control of the mind' becomes *yoga* only when the 'mind' is so far 'controlled' that it abides in its own pure form of consciousness.

The functions or operations of the *Chitta* (Mind) are fivefold —Right Cognition, Wrong Cognition, Supposition, Sleep, and Remembrance. Right Cognition is of three minds—Perceptional, Inferential and Verbal. Wrong Cognition is mistaken conviction brought about by some defect either in the cognitive agency or in the cognised object. Supposition (or Imposition) is distinguished from Wrong Cognition by the fact that while the latter is rectified by subsequent Right Cognition, the former is such that it persists all through worldly existence, just as tenaciously as any ordinary cognition; to this class belong all those popular errors of regarding Intelligence as a *quality* of the Soul, and so on. Remembrance is cognition brought about by impressions left by previous cognitions. By 'Sleep' is meant the cognition of pleasure that we have during sound sleep.

Yoga or Meditation is of two kinds—unconscious or *abstract* and conscious or *concrete*. In *Conscious* Meditation, also called *Salambana* or *Sabija*, the object meditated upon is distinctly or directly apprehended ; that is to say, in this meditation the inhibition of the mind enables the agent to directly apprehend the object on which he is meditating—for instance, some form of personal divinity. In Unconcious Meditation, also called *Niralambana* or *Nirbija*, on the other hand, there is a complete inhibition of all the functions of the mind, wherein the agent loses all consciousness of things outside himself; he is literally self-conscious, not indeed conscious of his self as apart from other *selves*, but of *the* Self and that alone as One, Absolute, Eternal, Unchanging. The effect of the former is visible or perceptible, consisting of the experiencing of desirable pleasures, and finally actually perceiving the Divinity; this last perception puts a stop to all kinds of pain, and thereby gradually leads to final Release. Unconcious Meditation also leads to final release; but immediately and directly; and it does not stand in need of any intervening processes.

This raises an interesting question: when the man has reached the stage of conscious meditation, what becomes of his past *Karma*—If he obtains final Release all at once, is all his Karma wiped off at one stroke? If not, how can he obtain perfect Release? The answer to this lies in the fact that *Karma* is divided into three classes—(1) the *Prârabdha* or *commenced*, those whose machinry has been set in motion towards their fruition in the present life; (2) the *Sanchita* or Accumulated—those that are lying latent, like seeds stocked up in the granary, for fruition in future lives; and (3) *Kriyamâṇa* or *Being done*,—those that are being done in the present life. Now there is nothing that can stop the machinery that has been set going; the tree that has sprouted must grow, to some extent at least,—the effects of the *Prârabdha karma* must be experienced. With regard to the *sanchita* however the case is different: the seeds may be deprived of their germinating power under the influence of extreme heat or cold; in the same manner the *accumulated* karma can be rendered ineffective by the force of wisdom. Lastly over the *kriyamâṇa* the agent has full control. Hence when the man reaches the stage of concious Meditation, he accelerates the fruition of his '*Prarabdha*' Karma, renders ineffective the '*sanchita*,' and being entirely free from personal desires, does not acquire any *dharma* or *adharma*, and thus has no *kriyamâṇa*; and the *Prârabdha Karma* being only limited, as soon as that has become exhausted, Release is attained. This is what happens in Conscious Meditation. Unconcious Meditation, on the other hand, is so powerful in its action that it tends to exhaust the Prârabdha also, not indeed, by wiping it off, but by making it ineffective by depriving it of such auxilliaries and aids during present life without which it cannot being about its effects. In fact this is what is meant by Karma being *destroyed* or *burnt*. As a matter of fact, in bringing about its results the Prârabdha stands in need of the aid of such auxilliaries as Ignorance, Egotism, Attachment and Longing after life, on the part of the agent; hence when the agent has by practice of meditation become free from these 'Obstacles' or 'Troubles',—he makes his Prarabdha entirely ineffective; and so attains Final Release immediately. In Conscious Meditation, there is some personal motive present, however pure, it may be; and so long as this is so, Egotism is there; and hence Prârabdha remaining effective, the Release is obtained, it is true,—but only after Prârabdha has become exhausted by actual experiencing of its results.

Of Conscious Meditation there are four kinds—which have been regarded as the four stages in the advancement towards meditation. All the four are not necessary for all men. If the aspirant has succeeded in reaching the higher stage he need not revert to the lower; and this for the simple reason that 'the ends of the latter will have been served by the former' (Yoga-Bhashya). Then again, all these four stages are to' be practised with reference to one and the same 'object of meditation'; as if one wavers from one to the other object the process will lose much of its force. With regard to the same object however the aspirant must proceed from the grosser or more easily perceptible aspects of it to the subtler or imperceptible aspects; and thus by the time he has passed through the four stages, the object is present before him in all its aspects.

These four kinds are—(1) the 'Argumentative,' whereby the aspirant is enabled to apprehend all the past, present and future aspects of the ordinary perceptible kind, of the object of his devotion–such f. i. as the elements and the sense-organs; (2) the Deliberative—whereby he is enabled to apprehend the ordinarily imperceptible aspects of that object; as for instance, Nature, Intelligence, Self-consciousness and the Rudimentary Elements. (3) the Joyous—whereby contemplating the object of devotion the aspirant feels a peculiar blissful sensation; and (4) the Selfconscious—whereby the aspirant comes to look upon himself as one with the object of devotion,

A distinction is made between what is called the *human* self,—which forms the twenty-fifth 'principle' in the constitution of the Universe, whereof Nature, Intelligence, Self-consciousness, the eleven organs, the five rudimentary elements and the five gross elements are the other twenty-four 'principles'—and the *Supreme Self*, on the ground that the latter is far more subtle than the former; as the human self is directly perceived in the aforesaid fourth stage of Conscious Meditation, while that of the Supreme Self we can have no direct knowledge; the only conception that we can have of it is what we may form out of our ideas of such qualities (if 'qualities' they can be called) as Absolute Unchangeability, Indivisibility and the like. The contemplation of the *self* (human) is possible during the aforesaid egoistic meditation; this is what is spoken of in Sankhya and Yoga works as 'Sattvapurushânyatâkhyâti' (the discernment of the distinction between the self and the other principles). The meditation of the supreme *Self* however is spoken of only in sutra I. 23.

It is not very easy to find what part this 'supreme self,' or 'God' plays in the cosmogony of Yoga. He is nowhere spoken of as the 'creator'; nor even as the consciousness permeating through all existence. He is spoken of only as an object of devotion, devotion to whom leads to highest results. In this respect the 'god' of the Yogin appears to hold the same position as the 'devatâ' of the Mimamsaka, who posits the 'devatâ' only as one to whom the prescribed sacrifices can be offered ; He has no other function at all. Later writers on Yoga were conscious of this; hence when dealing with the sutra defining God simply as 'that self which is ever untouched by the five kinds of troubles, Ignorance and the rest, as also by virtue, vice and their modifications' they proceeded to supplement this by additional accounts of the Godhead obtainable from other sources, chiefly Vedântic. For instance, Vijnana Bhiksha gives the following description :—'His powers and omniscience are equalled or excelled by none ; He is the Lord or Spiritual Chief and Father of all the gods, Brahma, Vishnu and Rudra; is the imparter of spiritual vision to the gods, in his character of the Inner Guide (Conscience ?) and also though the Vedas. Praṇava—'Om' is His name; Devotion to Him consists in contemplation of Him, beginning with the reciting of the Praṇava, and ending in the direct perception of His Effulgence. (Yogasârasangraha pp. 27-28.)

The 'Conscious' Yogin also has been classed under four heads, in accordance it would seem, with the above-mentioned four stages of Conscious Meditation : *viz* : : (1) The *Prathamakalpika*, one who is at the first stage, who is still practising the Argumentative form of meditation, wherein he looks upon all ordinary things of the world as true under ordinary conditions, and so forth. (2) the *Madhubhumika*—one occupying the honeyed or sweet stage—is one who has come to realise that the characters that he is generally accustomed to attribute to things are not real, but merely imposed upon them by usage; he looks upon the very essence of things, as free from all such impositions; for this reason he is called 'Ṛitamhbaraprajna' (of truth-supporting knowledge); and this stage is called 'Madhumati' (Honeyed) because it makes the aspirant feel extremely happy. (3) the 'Prajnâjyoti'—of bright Intelligence—who has won complete control over all subtle entities from Nature downwards; it is into this stage that the aforesaid 'Joyous' meditation enters. (4) the *Atikrântabhavaniya*—one who has passed beyond all that has to be experienced—is one who has reached the aforesaid 'self-conscious' meditation. The highest stage of this has been called '*Dharmamegha—Samadhi*' 'Cloud of Virtue'—which is thus described :—All desire for occult powers having been renounced, there immediately follows the discernment of the Self from Nature; and thus all Ignorance and consequent evils having disappeared, there appears in the mind of the aspirant a feeling of satiety, a sense of 'enough', with regard to all external things, gross and subtile alike ; this is the step that leads to the highest unconscious meditation and hence has been called 'Dharmamegha'—that which showers *dharma i.e.*, such virtue as omniscience and the like; when arrived at this stage the aspirant becomes a Jivanmukta, a Living Adept.

Abstract or Unconscious Meditation is of two kinds—the *Upâyapratyaya* and the *Bhavapratyaya*. The Upâyapratyaya Meditation is that which is accomplished by practice, *during present life*, of the various means prescribed in the Shâstras. Such means are faith, energetic concentration of the mind, constant contemplation, meditation and discernment born of Conscious Meditation. These five lead to Unconscious Meditation through Absolute Dispassion; and when all this is employed with great energy there then comes about Unconscious Meditation. But even though the agent is not sufficiently energetic, if he is devoted to God, he obtains the same results. 'Devotion to God' is a very potent factor in this, in as much as it puts an effective end to all evils that impede the progress of meditation. The *Bhavapratyaya* meditation is that which is accomplished during present life, but by force of practices carried on during preceding lives. This belongs to such persons as are either '*Videhas*'—*i. e.*, Bodiless Beings, such as Hiranyagarbha and the like, who carry on all their functions by means of the subtle body, and do not need the gross body—or '*Prakritilayas*,' or those who have attained to the position of the godhead after having worked up their way through the several 'coverings' or 'obstacles' to their upward progress, in the shape of Nature and its modifications. As this passage upward cannot be completed in only one life, it is not possible in the case of Conscious Meditation, which must come about as soon as its details have been fulfilled,—after which there is nothing to delay the accomplishment of the meditation; all this therefore being finished in a single life. It is for this reason that Conscious Meditation has not been divided into Upâyapratyaya and Bhavapratya: it is always Upâyapratyaya.

Though Unconcious Meditation is of the form of Inhibition, yet, while being practised, it develops in due course fresh powers and faculties at each step; and through these the Meditation develops itself in due time; as each faculty appears it reduces the force of opposing faculties tending to retard the required Inhibition of Mind, until true knowledge is finally attained. Thus it is that in the final stage of Unconcious Meditation all contending forces and faculties are laid at rest, and all evils having ceased, there remains no force in the opposing Prârabdha Karma of the aspirant. The mind thus having all its functions duly performed and inhibited, melts away along with all its products, into its source.

This absolute sleep of the mind constitutes the Isolation (Release) of the Self.

The reader who is interested in tracing unity among the diverse philosophical systems will be interested to find that writers on Yoga have tried to reconcile the view that Release is obtained by Meditation with the theory that it can be obtained by true knowledge alone. Both views are correct; both Yoga and Jnâna lead to release, each in its own way and independently of the other. But one who would seek to obtain it by means of true knowledge, would also have to practise that much of Concrete Meditation which leads to the discernment of the self from other things.

This closes our study of the first section. The second section deals with the *means*—Sâdhana—of Yoga.

Aspirants to Yoga are divided into three classes—(1) 'Ârurukshû'—'one desirous of climbing', (2) 'Yunjâna'—one engaged in the practice, and (3) 'Yogârudha'—one who has attained Yoga; and for each of these distinct means or methods are laid dawn. We may recall here the description of the last given in the Bhagavadgîtâ VI. 4 :—"One is said to be Yogârûdha when he ceases to become attached to any action or to any objects of sense, and when he has given up all desire for fruits of actions."

Those who belong to this highest class have passed through all the preliminary stages during their previous lives, and at once attain the highest Yoga; all that is needed for such people is constant Practice and Dispassion; they do not need the external diciplinary yoga. The 'Practice' meant here is the 'endeavour to fix the mind in unflinching concentration'; and 'Dispassion' is the feeling of 'enough' that one has with regard to objects of enjoyment; it is not mere absence of passion or attachment. It is of two kinds, the inferior kind having its origin in our knowledge of defects in the objects, and the higher consisting in our disregard for all such objects, not because of any. undesirable elements in them, but because of these being 'not self'.

As the means tending to the accomplishment of the aforesaid Exercise, the books lay down six methods called 'parikarma.' These are—(1) *Peace of mind,* brought about by friendly feelings towards happy beings, sympathy with the suffering, joyous regard for the virtuous and sympathetic disregard for the vicious;—(2) *Functioning towards objects*—consisting of the sensing of superphysical objects of sense;—(3) *Joyous Resplendent function*—tranquility of mind brought about by the recognition of Buddhi, and of the Self as distinct from it;—(4) *Contemplation of dispassioped minds*—of such people as Nârada and the like;—(5) *Looking upon ordinary cognitions as those of dream or sleep,*—and (6) *Contemplation of the object of worship in the form of some divinity.* Stress has not been laid upon the order in which the last two have to be practised. Practice and Dispassion are means to both Conscious and Unconscious Meditation.

For the second-class yogin, the Yunjâna, has been prescribed what may be called 'Diciplinary Yoga.' The highest form of this consists of—(1) *Religious Austerity,* the habituating of one's body to the bearing of the 'pairs of opposites',—(2) Study of works teaching Final Release, and silent repitition of the Praṇava and such other Mantras ;—and (3) Devotion to God—the offering of one's actions to the Lord, and the renouncing of all desire for fruits of actions.

The direct purpose served by this Diciplinary Yoga is the attenuation of the five *kleshas,* troubles or obstacles,—in the shape of—(1) Ignorance—the regarding of the non-eternal as eternal, (2) Egotism—the identifying of the Self with the not-self ;—(3) Affection—(4) Aversion,—and (5) Attachment to life—fear of death. These five have been called 'Viparyaya' by the Sankhyas, under the names respectively of—Tamas, Moha, Mahamoha, Tamisra, and Andhatamisra. Among them, Ignorance is the source of the other four. All these disturb the mind, and as such are impediments to Meditation. The attenuation of these lies in their being rendered incapable of putting obstacles in the way of right discernment of the Self from the Not-self.

The abovementioned Diciplinary Yoga purifies the mind, and thereby all chance for vice being removed, the cessation of vice is followed by the cessation of its effects in the form of Ignorance &c. All these—Ignorance and the rest—having been attenuated by the force of Diciplinary Yoga, the course of Right Discernment being no longer impeded, the Self comes to be rightly known ; there being no chance for the further operation of Ignorance and the other 'troubles,' the Agent arrives at the stage known as that of the 'Jîvanmukta.' He continues, however, to live for a while, in order to afford opportunity for the working up of his *prârabdha* Karma, on the exhaustion of which,—and on all the rest of his karma having been rendered inoperative by the absence of their necessary auxilliaries, Ignorance &c.,—there is no more need for the Self to be born again ; It therefore experiences no more pain—It is in the state of Absolute Bliss or Release.

When we understand the real source of 'bondage,' the process of 'Release' becomes more intelligible. As a matter of fact all virtue and vice are the result of Ignorance, Egotism, Affection, Aversion and Attachment to Life ; and we know also that it is only virtue and vice that are the sources of the *fruits* of past actions, in the shape of birth, experiences during life and so forth ; these experiences giving rise to pleasure and pain, the Self becomes bound up in these. When therefore, the root of all this evil, Ignorance, is destroyed by the right Discernment of the Self form the Not-self, all evils attendant upon that root-evil, cease forthwith. Thus there being no cause left, the effects, virtue and vice, cannot appear; and as these evils are necessary auxilliaries to the fruition of that portion of the past karma which has not been set in motion, all these latter are rendered ineffective ; and those already set in motion having been exhausted, there is no further occasion for the Self to undergo experiences,—whereupon it becomes 'free,' 'released.'

For the aspirant of the lowest class, the man of the ordinary life, there are eight 'means to yoga.' These are—(1) *Yama*, Restaint, consisting in harmlessness, truthfulness, respect for other's property, continence, and freedom from avarice, (2) *Niyama* or obligation, consisting of religious austerities. study, contentment, purity and adoration of god. These two have been regarded as purely extrinsic and as such chiefly purificatory in their character. (3) *Asana*, Posture ;—much undue importance has been attached to this factor of Yoga by later writers ; but Patanjali contents himself by the simple statement, that 'Posture' (for yoga) is that which is most conducive to fixity and comfort.' (4) Prâṇâyâma, Regulation of Breath—the effect of this is more or less physiological in character, 'physiology' pertaining also to the inner spiritual centres of energy. (5) *Pratyâhâra*, Abstraction, consists in the withdrawal of the mind and the sense-organs from their respective objects. These five have been regarded as 'external' factors, exercising a more or less exterior influence, dealing as they do with the controlling of the body, breathing and the senses. The next three have been called 'internal,' as exercising an inner influence, and hence of greater importance, bearing upon the mind directly. These are—(6) Dhâraṇâ, steadiness, fixing of the mind to a definite point in space occupied by the Divinity that forms the object of meditation,-such for instance as the lotus of the heart, the centre of the brain and so forth. (1) Dhyâna, contemplation, consists in the continuous flow of the conception of the object of meditation; when we have formed this conception, if it continues to occupy our mind, without any break, we are said to be 'contemplating.' (8) *Samâdhi*, Meditation Proper. When the aforesaid contemplation becomes free from all notions of difference (between the Agent himself, and the object of Meditation), and the mind becomes completely merged into the form contemplated, we have what has been called 'Samâdhi.

The third section deals with the Occult Powers. Though these have been described in detail, yet Patanjali definitely asserts that these are to be regarded as 'Powers' or Perfections only so long as the man is in the ordinary worldly state; they are great 'obstacles' in the way of the accomplishment of Pure Meditation :—'*Samâdhâvupasargâ vyutthâne siddhayah.*' These have been described with a view chiefly to show to the aspirant that even such sources of pleasure are not things to long for—they are as imperfect in their character as the ordinary pleasures of the world.

The fourth and the last section deals with Kaivalya or Mukti. This we have already explained above.

Bibliographical Information pertaining to the Yogasutra.

1. Yogasutras by Patanjali—printed with commentaries at Calcutta, Bombay and Benares.
2. Bhashya of Vyasa—commentary on (1) printed in Benares, Bombay Sanskrit Series, and Calcutta.
3. Tattvavaisharadi by Vachaspati Mishra commentary on No. (2)—printed along with it in Bombay Sanskrit Series, and also in Calcutta and Benares.
4. Pâtanjalarahasya—commentary on No. (3)—not printed. Mss. available.
5. Rajamartanda by Bhojadeva—a brief commentary on No. (1)—translated by Dr. Rajendralal Mittra, and printed in the Bibliotheca Indica.
6. Yogavartika by Vijnanabhiksu—commentary on (1) and parts of (2), printed in the 'Pandit.' Benares.
7. Yogamaniprabha Commentary on (1), printed in Benares
8. Yogachandrika—commentary on (1)—printed in Benares.
9. Nagesha Bhatta's commentary on (1)—printed in the 'Pandit'
10. Narayana Tirtha's commentary on (1)—not printed; available in Mss. This is a work of exceptional merit and usefulness.
11. English Translation of (1), with English commentary by M. N. Divedi—printed by the Bombay Theosophical Publishing Fund.
12. English Translation of (1) and (2), here offered to the public, and also in course of preparation by Mrs. Annie Besant and Bhagavan Dasa, and yet another by Dr. Woods (for the Harvard Oriental Series).
13. Hindi Translation of (1) and (2)—printed at Moradabad.

YOGA-DARŚANA.

THE SUTRAS OF PATANJALI—WITH THE BHÂSHYA OF VYÂSA.

WITH EXTRACTS FROM

THE TATTWAVAIS'ÂRADÎ OF VÂCHASPATI MIS'RA.

An English Translation—by GANGANATHA JHA, M.A.

SECTION I.

Com. :—May the resplendant Lord of Serpents, the many-hooded One, protect us,—He administering Yoga, while himself equipped with it, having a body of pure white, delighting in a serpentine body, the fountain-head of all wisdom, whose troubles are at an end, holding, as he does, terrific poison,—One who having renounced his original body, is born in this world for the manifold benefits of human-kind.

Sutra (*1*) :—Now (begins) the exposition of Yoga.

Com. :—*Atha* denotes '*Adhikâra*' *i. e.* the commencement of a topic. (The meaning of the *Sutra* being :) The Science of the instruction of Yoga is to be understood to have begun (here).

Yoga is *Samâdhi*, Meditation ; but (this meditation) is a property of the internal organ, common to all its various stages. The stages or states of the internal organ are: (1) The Fickle (*Kshipta*), (2) The Infatuated (*Mugdha*), (3) Voluptuous or Distracted (*Vikshipta*), (4) The One-pointed (*Ekâgra*), and (5) The Controlled (*Niruddha*). From among these, the meditation in the Voluptuous or Distracted state of the internal organ, being subordinate to the voluptuousness or distraction, has no place on the side of Yoga (proper). That (meditation) however which belongs to the one-pointed internal organ, enlightening the true and agreeable object, destroying the troubles, loosening the bonds of action, and bringing one face to face with Control proper—such meditation is called the Conscious (*Samprajnâta*) Yoga. This is attended by Argumentation, Deliberation, Joy and Egoism.

The entire subjugation of all the functions (of the internal organ) constitutes what is called Unconscious or Abstract (*Asamprajnâta*) Yoga.

Notes :—At the outset it may be stated that the translation follows the interpretation of Vâchaspati Mis.a, modified in places by that of Vijnâna Bhikshu.

" *Yoganusâsana*"—Dr. Rajendra Lal Mitra has been apparently misled by a wrong reading of the Bhâshya—having read it as " *yoganus'âsànam*" *nam sâstram*," he makes the commentator explain the word ("*yogâ'nusàsana*") as being the specific name of the work. There is no " *nàma*" in the Bhâshya. however; hence the meaning of the Bhâshya is as given in the translation. If however we accept Dr. Mitra's reading (and it is by no means a bad reading), his interpretation would be the most appropriate. But Vâchaspati Misra evidently rejects this reading; using, as he does, the root meaning of the word *anusâsana*, to point to the prior authorship of Hiranyagarbha, with regard to the science of Yoga. It is remarkable that Dr. Mirta should have overlooked this fact when quoting from the *Tattwa-vais'âradi*

" *Vêditayvam*" ("to be understood") by the disciples (Vij-Bhikshu). This word is made by Vâchaspati Misra to mean that though the object to be explained is Yoga (practical) and not the science, yet the pupil is to *understand* the latter as the topic taken in hand, because practical Yoga itself can be explained only by means of the science; and as such the final aim of the exposition comes to be practical Yoga itself.

" *Sa Châ &c.*" *Cha*=*tu* (but). Though etymologically the word *yoga*=*Samadhi*, yet this latter is only a part of Yoga (as will be explained later on). " *Stages*"—The *Madhumati* and the rest, to be explained below. 'Meditation' (*Samâdhi*) is only the root-meaning of the word *yoga*, the real meaning being 'the suppression of the functions of the internal organ.'

" *Property of the internal organ*"—this is added in order to set a side the view that the functions belong to the Spirit. *Chitta* is *Buddhi*, the Internal Organ; for certainly no cognition can belong to the unchanging eternal Intelligence (*Chiti-S'akti*).

The *Kshipta* abounds in Rajas, the *Mugdha* in Tamas, and the *Vikshipta* in Sattwa. The *One-pointed* or *Concentrated* state is that in which all the functions of the internal organ have ceased, and only the *Sanskara* (residue of the actions) is left behind.

"*True and agreeable object*" ("*Saddhûtam artham*")—The particle *Bhûta* precludes all superimposed (and hence false) objects; and "*Sat*" is employed in order to preclude the functions of Sleep which abound in Tamas, and as such, causing pain, cannot be called "agreeable."

"*Enlightening.*"—The prefix *pra* denotes *direct* perception.

In order to define the Yoga above mentioned we the next aphorism—

Sutra (2):—Yoga is the suppression of the functions of internal organ.

Com.:—Since the word 'all' does not appear before 'functions, *Conscious* or Concrete meditation also becomes included in the name '*yoga*.'

The internal organ is made up of three attributes,—in as much as it has the characters of truth, activity and inertia. *Sattwa* in the form of the internal organ, when intermixed with Rajas and Tamas, comes to be attached to power and the objects (of sense). Sattwa again, when mixed up with Tamas, tends towards sin, ignorance, non-dispassion (or attachment) and non-power (or weakness). The same Sattwa 'lastly everywhere shinning, on having its covering of illusion removed, when tinged by Rajas, tends towards virtue, knowledge, dispassion and power. The same Sattwa however, when passed beyond the taint of Rajas, fixed in its own form, consisting purely of discriminative knowledge of Matter and Spirit, tends towards contemplation, called "Cloud of Virtue." This is what is called "Supreme Contemplation" by the Dhyánis.

The Sentient Faculty (or Intelligence proper), the Unchanging and the Immobile—having the objects presented to Itself, is pure and endless; and It consists in the attribute of Sattwa. For this reason discriminative knowledge is contrary to this (since such knowledge is modifiable, mobile, non-intelligent, finite and impure).

For this reason, the internal organ—having become indifferent to the sentient faculty, (naturally) suppresses the aforesaid discriminative knowledge; and when in this condition, it centres itself in mere residuum (*Sanskara*). This is "Seedless Meditation"—and because nothing else is cognised in this state, therefore it is called "Unconscious" or Abstract (*asamprajnâta*).

Thus is Yoga—of the form of the suppression of the functions of the internal organ—two-fold.

Notes:—"*Functions*" Pramâna and the rest are to be described hereafter. "*All*"—If Yoga were defined as the suppression of *all* the functions &c., then Conscious Meditation would be excluded; because such meditation is not totally free from such functions of the internal organ as abound in pure Sattwa. The definition given however includes this Meditation also, in as much as there too we have the suppression of the functions of Rajas & Tamas.

"*Truth &c.*"—representing Sattwa, Rajas and Tamas respectively. These characteristics however imply the others also—viz, happiness and buoyancy (of Sattwa), remorse and unhappiness (of Rajas), and sluggishness (of Tamas). This three-fold character of the internal organ is laid down in order to explain the three stages of it mentioned above. (The *Kshipta &c.*)

"*Intermixed with Rajas and Tamas*"—in equal quantities. This represents the Distracted (*Vikshipta*) stage.

"*When mixed up with Tamas*"—representing the Infatuated (*mugdha*) stage.

"*Ignorance*"—Mistaken knowledge.

"*Tinged with Rajas*"—representing the Active (*Kshipta*) state.

"*Passed beyond the taint &c.*"—Representing the fourth stage of the internal organ. Here ends the application of the definition to Conscious Meditation.

"*The Sentient faculty &c.*"—This laying down of the propriety of the sentient faculty and the impropriety of discriminative knowledge serves as an introduction to the supreme suppressive (unconscious) Meditation which leads to the rejection of discriminative knowledge, and the acceptance of the Sentient Faculty pure and simple.

"*Pure*"—because free from impurities in the shape of pleasure, pain and the like.

"*Having objects presented to herself*"—This is added in order to meet the objection that 'the sentient faculty (1) cognising the various objects of sense and (2) accepting and rejecting the various forms of such objects,—

cannot be said to be either pure or endless'. The objection would have held good if the sentient faculty took upon itself the various forms &c. But such is not the fact; it is Buddhi, the internal organ, which assumes the various forms of the objects of sense, and presents these as such to the sentient faculty, which latter being by its very nature immobile, is untouched by these. The possibility of such cognition by a Faculty itself untouched by the objects, will be explained later on.

"*For this reason &c.*"—From here begins the application of the definition to Unconscious Meditation.

"*Seed-less*"—devoid of the seeds, Birth, life and experience &c.

The definition of Yoga then comes to be this: Yoga is that particular state of the internal organ, in which its functions (in the form of Pramâna and the rest) have been suppressed.

The internal organ being in that condition—and as such there being a complete absence of objects,—what is the character of the Purusha—being as it is of the nature of the cognition of Buddhi (the internal organ)?

Reply:—

Sutra (3):—Then there is an abiding of the spectator in its own form.

Com.:—"The abiding in its own form" is *then*, as in beatitude (identical with) the sentient faculty. In the (ordinary) waking state however, the sentient faculty, though being the same, is not (exactly) the same.

Notes:—The present Sutra is introduced in order—(1) to show the motive for the said Yoga. (2) to complete the definition of Yoga, and (3) to show the unchanging character of the Purusha.

The sense of the question may be thus rendered, in the words of Vijnâna Bhikshu: "When the internal organ is in the condition of Abstract Meditation, then in what character does the Purusha stand—being as it is of the form of the cognition of Buddhi, *i. e.* its witness? Does it even then, as in the ordinary waking state, stand in the form of illuminiation (*prakâs'a*),—its non-perception being due to the absence of objects? or does it then become, like a log of wood, non-illuminating?" The aphorism replies, admitting the former of these two alternatives.

"*Then*"—during Abstract Meditation,—and not during the ordinary waking state.

"*As in beatitude*"—This is added in order to shew that the motive is no other than the removal of pain in the form of the functions.

"*In the waking &c.*"—This is added in anticipation of the following objection: "The sentient faculty abiding in its form during meditation, brings about absence of pain and non-abiding in it in the ordinary state, and as such bringing about pain, would become modifying; and if such a difference were set aside, there would be an identity between the meditative and the waking states." The sense of the reply is that the unchanging sentient faculty never swerves from its nature, but continues the same in all the states—waking or meditative. The only difference however is, that in the waking state, the Intelligence does not shine so well as it does during Meditation or Beatitude.

"*Abiding &c.*"—The unconditioned and pure form of the Purusha is pure intelligence (a sentient faculty),—the calm and the active &c. due to the predominance of the one or the other of the attributes being only its conditioned form, like the redness of the crystal due to its proximity to a red flower; as the crystal regains its pure whiteness on the removal of the red object, so on the removal of the functions of the internal organ, does the Purusha regain its unalloyed abiding in its nature. The unchanging Purusha is of the nature of pure light, during meditation, as well as during the waking state.

In comparison with Abstract Meditation, Concrete Meditation is to be taken along with the waking state.

How then? On account of the objects having been presented,—

Sutra (4):—At other times, conformity to the functions.

Com.:—In the waking state the functions of the Purusha are indentical with those of the internal organ. Hence the *Sutra*: "Perception is one and cognition or knowledge is Perception."

The internal organ, like the magnet, affecting by mere proximity, being the object of perception, becomes the self of the Purusha, the Lord. Therefore the cause of the Purusha's perception of the functions of the internal organ is its eternal connection therewith.

Notes:—"*At other times*"—In the waking state.

"*Identical &c.*"—That is to say—as in the case of the crystal and the red flower, so in that of the Purusha and the internal organ, close proximity leads to a notion of identity; and this leads to the imposition of the functions of the internal organ on the Purusha—e. g. "I am happy &c." Though this imposition too is only a function of the internal organ, and as such does not affect the true nature of the Purusha, yet the presentation of the Purusha in the colours of the internal organ leads to the notions of 'wrongness' 'agency,' 'discriminative wisdom' &c., with regard to the Purusha, which is, by its very nature, free from all these. This point is dealt with at lenght in IV-22 and III-34.

"*Hence the Sutra &c.*"—This Sutra is attributed by Vâchaspati Misra as well as by Vidnyâna Bhikshu, to Panchasikha Achârya, the great master of Sânkhya.

The question started by the first part of this Sutra is—How can the perception be *one* and the same, in the case of the internal organ and that of the Purusha? For, the perception of the internal organ is no other than the function with regard to the various objects of sense and to discriminative knowledge,—a function inferred to be insentient on account of its owing its origin to insentient Nature; whereas the perception of the Purusha must be other than this—being simple cognition in the form of pure intelligence.

To this the second part replies—"Cognition is Perception." The Sameness or oneness spoken of is with regard to the fleeting (appearing and disappearing) cognition, to which the term is ordinarily applied. Intelligence is the Purusha's nature, not its cognition (as the question presupposes), amenable as it is to inference from sacred texts, and not to ordinary perception. By this it is shown that in the waking state the final cause is Ignorance, which also leads to the connection of the Purusha with the internal organ, which in its turn leads to the idea (in the Purusha) of ownership, and thence of experience (pleasure and pain).

"*The internal organ like the magnet &c.*"—This is added in anticipation of the objection that the fact of the connection of the internal organ with the Purusha helping towards the experience of the latter, would prove the modifying character of the Purusha. The sense of the Bhâsha is that the internal organ is not in contact with the Purusha, but only in proximity with it; and this proximity too is neither in space nor in time, (becauee Purusha is unconnected with these, being eternal and omnipresent), but only in the form of *Capability*. And the faculty of experience (of the Purusha), and that of being the object of experience (of the internal organ) cannot be denied; with this last point in view it is added—"*being the object of perception*" *i. e.* having developed into the form of the various objects of sense, Sound &c.—and as such becoming objects of experience.

"*Of the purusha*"—Though experience, being of the form of the objects of sense, is really a function of the internal organ, yet it is spoken of here as belonging to the Purusha, on account of the identity of the functions of the two (in the waking state).

Thus it is proved that though there is no real contact of the Purusha with the internal organ, yet there applies to it the character of participating in the benefits offered by the internal organ, as also that of being unchanging.

"*The Cause of the Purusha's &c*".,—This is added in anticipation of the following objection: "The idea of ownership, leading to experience, has been said to be due to Ignorance,—but to which cause do you attribute the action of this Ignorance? There must be some cause for this." The sense of the reply is that the cause is no other than an (hypothetical) eternal connection (between the eternal Purusha and the eternal Ignorance), which is like the relation of the seed and the sprout.

The internal organ being manifold, the objects of suppression,

Sutra (5):—the functions, are five-fold, painful (and) non-painful.

Com:—The "painful" are causes of pain—the fruitful ground for the aggregate of the karmic residua. And the "non-painful" have knowledge for their object, and are opposed to the action of the Attributes. The non-painful ones falling in the current of the painful ones, though occurring within two painful ones, are still non-painful; similarly are the painful ones, occurring among non-painful ones, called "painful."

Residua of one kind are those brought about by the functions of the same kind, and also the functions by the residu—this wheel of function and residua is incessantly revolving.

Thus the internal organ, having attained to this condition, and its action having ended, stands equal to the Spirit, or is dissolved.

These functions being painful, and non-painful, are five-fold.

Notes.—"*Kleśahetukah*" is explained by Vachaspati Misra as also meaning —"caused by the troubles—Asmitā &c." "*Knowledge*"—Knowledge discriminative of the Spirit and the Attributes; hence "opposed to the action of the Attributes."

"*The painful ones falling &c.*"—This is added, in order to meet the following objection: "All individuals being born with passions and attachments, they are all possessed only of the painful functions; and no non-painful ones are possible among a host of the other kind; consequently to assert that the painful functions are suppressed by the non-painful ones, and these latter again by the higher Dispassio 1, is a mere waste of words. Vijnana Bhikshu however explains it as anticipating the following objection. "The author of the aphorisms has laid down the advisability only of the Dark (the painful) and the Good (the non-painful) functions, and he has altogether ignored those of a mixed character." The reply serves to include these latter in the two mentioned in the aphorism.

"*Residua &c.*"—With a view to describe the effects of the functions of the internal organ, the commentator begins here with the mention of the cause of the troubles of Re-birth.

"*Of one kind &c.*"—The two kinds here spoken of are the 'painful' and the 'non-painful.'

"*Thus the internal &c.*"—*Thus i.e.* being of the nature of the karmic cycle.

"*In this condition.*"—Having been suppressed *i.e.* during meditation.

"*Is turning*"—Till the completion of the suppression.

"*Stands equal to the spirit*"—This in the case of a living adept—the *Jivanmukta.*

"*Is dissolved*"—In the case of the ordinary beatitude. The former disappearance of the internal organ is called its *Sarupanâśa* (*i.e.*, the destruction of the internal organ with its form), and the latter the *Arupanâśa* (without form).

Sutra (6):—Right Notion, Misconception, Fancy, Sleep and Memory.

Com:—Among these (*i.e.* the five-fold functions of the internal organ just named)—

Sutra (7):—Perception, Inference, Testimony are the right Notions.

Com:—The internal organ being affected by the external object through the path-way of the sense-organs, there arises a functioning thereof, having the aforesaid external thing for its object, and having as its principal concern the ascertainment of a certain specific aspect of the object, which naturally partakes of the generic as well as of the specific. Such a function constitutes the Right Notion, called *Perception.* The effect of this Right Notion is the cognition of the function of the internal organ—the cognition belonging to the Spirit, and being co-ordinate or identical (with the Buddhi). The Spirit is the joint-cogniser with the internal organ. This we shall explain later on.

Of the object of inference there is a certain relationship which is common to all homogenous objects, and dissociated from the heterogenous ones ; the function, having this relation for its object, concerned chiefly with the ascertainment of the generic (character of things), is *Inference.* As for example—The planets have motion, because they approach different regions, like Chaitra ;—the Vindhya Mountain having no such approach, has no motion.'

A certain object, having been either perceived or inferred by an authoritative person, is verbally expressed for the sake of transferring that cognition to another person. The function having, through words, such a thing for its object, is Testimony for the listener. That Testimony fails which is based on the assertion of an untrustworthy speaker, who has neither seen nor inferred an object truly. If however, the original speaker has seen and inferred an object truly, then the testimony becomes infallible.

Notes: (1) " *Cognition of the function of the internal organ* "—The form of the function is —" *This is a jar* ;" whereas that of the cognition is—'*I perceive the jar.*'

(2) " *Is co-ordinate or identical &c.*"—This is added in anticipation of the following objection : 'The cognition being in the Spirit, it cannot be the effect of a function of the internal organ.' The sense of the reply is that the cognition of the Spirit is not *produced* ; what happens is that the intelligence of the Spirit, being reflected in the mirror of the internal organ, is stamped with the character of the objective form then predominating in the *Buddhic* function. Thus then, this intelligence being identical with the internal organ, with which again the function is identical,—both come to have a common substrate ; and as such the cognition of the Spirit is quite rightly said to be the effect of the function (*Vide* Aph. I—4.)

(3) " *Having as its principal concern &c.*"—This serves to differentiate Perception from Inference. Though the generic character of things also, appears in Perception, yet this is always subordinated to the specific.

This definition of Perception implies direct cognition of all kinds, thus applying also to discriminative knowledge.

" *Joint Cogniser*."—In anticipation of the following objection :—

'All external percepation has been seen to be of the form of the object; Spirit on the other hand, being unchanging, can never take any objective form; under these circumstances, how can the Spirit be said to be the witness of the function of the internal organ ? Or, secondly, how can the cognition of the Spirit be identical with the said function ?' The sense of the reply is that though the real cogniser is the internal organ, yet the Spirit becomes its co-partner (in the manner explained in note 2.)

(4) " *Later on* "—i.e. *in Sutra* IV. 21.

(5) " *Common to the homogenous* "—This differentiates the definition from all kinds of Contradictory Inference.

(6) " *Dissociated from the heterogenous* "—This sets aside the *Too Broad General* and *Partial* Inferences.

(7) " *Relationship* "—This relationship is constituted by the Middle Term, the mark or the characterestic.—This sets aside the Incomplete Inference.

(8) " *concerned Chiefly &c.*"—This differentiates the given definition from *Perception.*

(9) " *An authoritative person* "—The authority, meant here, implies the possession of the knowledge of truth, mercy, and the extreme subtlesensitiveness of the sense-organs.

(10) " *If the original speaker &c.*"—This is added in order to validate the authority of the *Smritis*, where the original speaker is said to be God Himself.

Sutra (8): Misconception is false notion, abiding in a form, which is not that (of the object).

Com:—This is not a right notion ; because, it is always set aside by right notion, which has for its object something really existing in the external world. It has been always seen that a right notion always sets aside a wrong one; *e.g.* the perception of the double moon is set aside by the subsequentive of the single moon.

It is this that constitutes the five-fold Illusion or Nescience:—(1) Ignorance, (2) Egotism, (3) Attachment, (4) Envy, and (5) Tenacity of life—the five Troubles. These five have also the respective names of : (1) *Tamas* (Darkness), (2) *Moha* (Illusion), (3) *Mohumoha* (Great Illusion,), (4) (*Timisra*)and (5) *Andhatamisra*. The (Blinding Darkness) This will be defined in connection with the impurities of the internal organ.

Notes : (1) " *Abiding &c.*,"—This includes " Doubt."

(2) " *False notion* "—Serves to set aside " Fancy;" because people ordinarily act professedly in accordance with " Fancy," but never with " False Notion."

(3) " *Ignorance &c.*"—Cf. *Sânkhya-Karika*.

"भेदस्तमसोऽष्टविधो मोहस्य च दशविधो महामोहः।
" तामिस्रोऽष्टादशधा तथा भवत्यन्धतामिस्रः ॥

Sutra (9):—*Fancy* is (a notion) founded on a knowledge conveyed by words, but of which there is no object (corresponding in reality).

Com: This cannot be included either within Right Notion, or within Misconception. Because though it has got no object corresponding in reality, yet its acceptance in usage is seen to be based on the power of the knowledge of words. As for example, the assertion—" Intelligence is the form of the Spirit." If the Spirit is nothing more than intelligence, then what would be named and qualified by what? It is only when there is such nomination or qualification that we have the function.—*e. g.* " Chaitra's cow." *Similarly*—" The Spirit, having all objective properties alienated from it, is devoid of action; " and—" *Bâna* sits, will sit, and sat. " With regard to absence of motion, however, only the meaning of the root is signified. Similarly again, " Spirit has the property of non-production",—the qualifying adjunct here implying merely the negation of production, and not any property belonging to the Spirit: and for this reason, (in the example given) the qualification is a *fancied* one, on which the said usage is based

Notes:—(1) " *This cannot &c.*"—This is added in order to guard against the possibility of Fancy being included in Testimony, (because based on a knowledge of words), or in Misconception (because devoid of an object). The two qualifications in the Sutra are such that the first precludes Fancy from Misconception, and the second from Right Notion.

(2) *If the Spirit &c.*—The meaning of this is: Sometimes difference is perceived in identity, and at others identity in difference; and Fancy consisting in the appearance of such false difference and identity, cannot be said to be Right Notion; nor can it be called Misconception, because that would go against usage.

(3) " *What* " and " *What &c.*"—The object qualified, and, the qualification. Because there can be no qualification, when the qualified and the qualifier are identical.

(4) " *We have the function* "—*i.e.* function in the shape of signification by sentence,—the verbal signification.

(5) " *Similarly &c.*"—Another example of Fancy.

(6) " *Objective properties* "—Such as mobility &c. belonging to earth and the other like external objects.

(7) " *Devoid of action* "—This is called *Fancy*, because according to the Sânkhya there can be no property of the character of mere negation; and as such the property mentioned cannot be said to belong to the Spirit.

(8) " *Bâna sits &c.*"—The third example (a popular one). In the sentence " *Bâna Sits &c,*" what is implied by ' sits &c.' is a mere sequence of time, as in the case of " he cooks."

(9) " *With regard to the absence of motion &c.*"—This is said in anticipation of the following assertion of the objector—" All right, we may accept the qualification of the '*bâna*' by the action of '*sitting*' (with the aforesaid sequence of time), which is certainly other than the *bâna* itself." The sense of the reply according to Vijnana Bhikshu is that in the case of the Fancy with regard to the " absence of motion," the only real signification consists in the meaning of the root qualified by the various tenses. The 'nominative agency,' and 'the tense with reference to the agency' &c. are all fancied; because the action of the form of 'absence of motion' cannot belong to the *bâna*. Vâchaspatimisra however explains thus:—" The absence of itself is assumed in the first place, then follows a whole series of assumptions with regard to its affirmative character, and the sequence of time with reference to it."

(10) " *Similarly &c.*"—This last example is cited with the following fact in View:—" The assumed negation, like affirmation, appears as if referring to all the Spirits; and it is not a property apart from the Spirit itself."

Sutra (10):—Sleep is the function having for its object the conception of negation.

Com:—And this is a particular kind of conception, because it is recalled in the waking state How? In this manner: "(1) I have slept well; my happy mind brightens my intellect. (2) I have slept ill; my mind wandering listlessly, has become worthless. (3) I have slept like a log of wood; my limbs are heavy; and my tired mind is lazy and seems to be absent.' This recalling by a person on waking would not have been, if there were no knowledge of any conception; the reminiscences connected with sleep could not have the conception for their object. Therefore Sleep is a particular conception; and this too, like all other conceptions, ought to be suppressed during meditation.

Notes:—"*Recalling*"—*i.e.* (in all its details). These details are exemplified in the following sentences.

(2) "*I have slept &c*"—The three kinds of sleep described owe their difference to the preponderance of one or other of the three attributes during sleep *e.g.* The first shows a preponderance of *Sattwa* over *Rajas* and *Tamas* (2) that of *Rajas* over *Sattwa* and *Tamas*, and (3) that of *Tamas* over the other two.

(3) "*Ought to be suppressed*"—Because abounding in *Tamas* it is contradictory to both kinds of meditation.

Sutra (11):—Memory is the non-relinquishment of an object that has been cognised.

Com:—Does the internal organ remember the cognition, or the object? The cognition,—coloured by the cognised (object), and (as such) manifesting (or illuminating) the forms of both the cognised (object) and the cognition,—produces an impression, (*sanskára*) of the *same character*. And this impression, being of the same form as its cause, brings about a recollection of the same character, partaking of both the cognised and the cognition.

Of these, the cognition has got the form of the cognition for its principal factor; and Memory or Recollection has got the form of the cognised for its precedent.

This *Memory* is two-fold—(1) One whose object to be remembered is *assumed*, and (2) the other whose object *is not assumed*. During a dream we have the former, whereas in the waking state, we have the latter.

All kinds of Memory owe their existence to the prior experience of Right Notion, Misconception, Fancy, Sleep and Memory.

All these functions are constituted by pleasnre, pain and illusion. These three will be explained under '*Klesa*'. Attachment belongs to pleasure and envy to pain; while bellusion is ignorance. All these functions are to be suppressed—their suppression leading to one of the two sorts of Meditation.

Notes:—(1) Memory differs from the preceding functions in this that the aforesaid functions lead to the cognition of strong and unseen objects, whereas Memory can never go beyond the field of past experience.

(2) " *Of the same character*"—*i. e.* Partaking of the character of the *cognise* as well as the *cognition*.

(3) " *Of these, the cognition &c.*"—*Grahana* (literally) = Holding, or accepting; and certainly no holding is possible of an object already held; consequently the characteristic of the cognition here noted, implies the province of cognition (*pratyaya or Jnana*) to be restricted to strange and unseen objects. The use of the word *Buddhi* is here ambiguous. Here it = *Jnâna*; and not *antahkarana*, as usual.

(4) "*Memory has got &c.*"—This *precedence* of the cognised object is the same as the fact of its having already been the object of some foregoing function. Thus then the definition of Memory comes to be the function having for its object something that has already been the object of a foregoing function. And this is the " non-relinquishment" (of an object already cognised by a foregoing function) mentioned in the aphorism.

(5) "*This Memory is two-fold*"—This is added in order to meet the assertion that in a dream memory is found to be touching unknown regions. The sense of the reply that what we find in a dream is not real recollection but only a semblance thereof.

(6) " *Assumed*"—*i. e.* not really existing.

What is the means for the suppression of these?

Sutra (12):—By Exercise and Dispassion, (follows) their suppression.

Com:—The river of the internal organ flows both ways. It flows for good, and it flows for evil. That which has its mouth at Isolation, and its bottom in Discrimination, flows for good. Where-as the one having its mouth at Rebirth and its bottom in Non-discrimination, flows for evil. Among these, the flow of (worldly) objects is thinned by Dispassion; and the flow of discrimination is opend by the Exercise of discriminative vision. Thus we see that the suppression of the functions of the internal organ is dependent upon both of these.

Notes. :—" *Having its mouth &c.*"—*i.e.* Having its end in Isolation and its current flowing through discrimination of Spirit from Matter.

(2) " *Thinned.*"—Damned *i.e.* stopped.

Sutra (13):—Exercise is the effort towards quietness.

Com:—"Quietness" (*Sthiti*) is the calm flow of the internal organ clear of its functionings. And Exercise consists in an effort for this *i.e.* an undaunted *courageous* and spirited endeavour, consisting in acting upto the means of attaining the aforesaid calmness.

Notes :—(1) " *Clear of its functionings*"—*i.e.* of the Foul and Dark functions. This is added by the commentator in consideration of Concrete Meditation which abounds in Goodness.

(2) " *Acting upto the means*"—The means are Restraint and the rest to be described in Sec, II.

Sutra (14) :—But it is of firm ground when attended to for a long time unremittingly and with proper devotion.

Com. :—Being attended to for a long time, and unremittingly—and brought about by penance, celibacy, knowledge and faith, and as such endowed with proper devotion—it becomes steadfast; that is to say, its object is not then easily suppressed by the impressions of the agitative stage.

Notes :—(1) The "*but*" of the aphorism points to the following difficulty in the mind of the author: Exercise being bound up with its eternal contradictory, the impressions of the Agitation stage, how can it lead to calmness? In reply, the aphorism lays down the steady character of exercise when accompained by the qualifications herein enumerated.

Sutra (15):—Dispassion is the (*Vaśikárasanjná*) Consciousness of being the subjugator, belonging to one who is devoid of any thirst for perceptible and scriptural objects.

Com. :—When one becomes devoid of any desire for the temporal perceptible objects—women, food drink and wealth,—and for the scriptural objects–the attainment of heaven, dis-embodiment, dissolution in Nature,—then his internal organ, noticing the objective discrepancies even in the relation of celestial and terrestrial objects, attains to the name of *Vaśikárasanjnà* which, on the strength of the recognition of discrepancies, is of the nature of अनाभोग, *i.e.*, free from all faults of attachment. (And this *Vaśikárasanjná* or consciousness of being the subjugator, is Dispassion.)

Notes :—(1) The internal organ, noticing the discrepancies, becomes indifferent to the various objects of sense, and to this indifference is given the name of *Vaśikarasajnà*.

(2) "*Discrepancies of objects*"—*i.e.*, the fact of their being subject to the three kinds of pain.

The other kinds of Dispassion will be described later on.

Sutra (16):—Indifference to the attributes, being conducive to the knowledge of the Spirit, is the highest (form of it).

Com. :—(1) The agent who recognises discrepancies in temporal and spiritual objects, and hence becomes dispassionate, and (2) one whose internal organ has been calmed by supreme discrimination due to the purity of spiritual exercise, and who has hence become detached from the attributes constituting the manifested and the unmanifested forms of matter;—these two indicate the two kinds of Dispassion. Of these, the latter is the sole effulgence of wisdom, on the appearance of which, the agent equipped with knowledge, reflects thus: "I have attained to what I had to attain,—the objects to be destroyed, the troubles, have been destroyed,—cut off is the thickly interwoven chain of metemspsychosis, whose unbroken range causes the death of the born and the birth of the dead."

Dispassion is the highest stage of knowledge; and the necessary concomittant of this alone, is Isolation.

Notes: (1) "*Purity*"—Freedom from Foulness and Darkness.

(2) "*One whose internal organ &c*"—This qualification is what is technically called "Cloud of Virtue."

(3) "*Two kinds of Dispassion.*"—The first form is possible when the internal organ is left contaminated with a particle of Foulness, having all Darkness completely washed away by the excess of Goodness. This may belong even to the *Taushtikas* (those whose aim ends in the nine forms of contentment), who thereby attain to "dissolution into nature." [Cf. *Sánkhyakárikâ*: "*Vairágyát prakritilaygah* &c. &c.."

(4) *Sole effulgence of wisdom*"—The egpithet "sole" precludes all objectivity from this Dispassion. This second form is free even from the slightest contamination of Foulness, and hence rests glorying in pure Goodness. Hence its "Effulgence." Though effulgence forms the very nature of the internal organ, yet as this latter abounds in the impurities of Foulness and Darkness, the effulgence becomes shrouded. When however the impurities have been washed off, there is full effulgence, all in all.

(5) "*Equipped with knowledge*"—Resting in the meditation, "cloud of virtue," on the attainment of spiritual effulgence just spoken of.

(6) "*What I had to attain*"—*i.e.*, Isolation; because under the circumstances, there is only the impression, deprived of its root.

(7) "The objects to be destroyed &c."—The following assertions are the reasons for the proceeding declaration. *Vide* II-12, II-13, IV-29 and IV-31.

Question:—"When the agent has suppressed his internal organ through the two means (just described), how can the meditation be said to be *Conscious*?"

(*Answer*):—

Sutra (17):—Conscious, because attended with the forms of argumentation, deliberation, joy, and egoism.

Com.:—(1) "Argumentation" is the gross perception of the internal organ, with regard to its object; whereas (2) "Deliberation" is subtle in its nature. (3) "Joy" is delight. (4) "Egoism" is the partial cognition of identity.

Of these, the first followed by the other four constitutes the Argumentative Meditation; the second, devoid of Argumentation, the Deliberative; the third without Deliberation the Joyful. The fourth without this, is purely Egoistic. All these forms of meditation are concrete.

Notes:—(1) "*Gross perception*"—the "perception" is called "gross" because the objects are such. Such objects are the Gods contemplated as having four arms, yellow cloth &c. &c.

(2) "*Subtle*"—*i.e.* Deliberation has for its objects the subtle primary elements, and the rest.

(The first two refer to the *perceived*)

(3) "*Joy*"—refers to the *instrument* (the senses). The perception of the internal organ with regard to the gross senses, constitutes "Joy." The senses are the products of Self-consciousness in which the attribute of Goodness predominates; and goodness is pleasant; therefore the senses are also pleasing; consequently the perception by means of these is "Joyous."

(4) "*Cognition of partial of identity*"—this describes meditation with regard to the perceiver.

Now, what is the nature of Unconscious or Abstract meditation and what are the means to it ?

Reply:—

Sutra (18):—The other, preceded by the practice of the cause of suspension, is that in which the residua alone remain behind.

Com:—When all the functions have been suspended and the residua alone remain behind, then we have a supression of the internal organ, which constitutes (a form of) meditation, called the *Unconscious* or *Abstract*.

Of this the means is the highest] form of Dispassion (*see above*). And, because an exercise based on an object would not be capable of being fit for its accomplishment, therefore the objectless (or immaterial) cause of suspension is made the basis here ; and this cause is devoid of any material object. (Consequently) the internal organ, preceded by the practice thereof, becomes immaterial, as if non-existing. This Immaterial or seedless meditation is what is called the Unconscious or the Abstract.

Notes: (1) "*Suspension*"—*i.e.* of the functions.

(2) "*Preceded by*"—Caused or brought about by.

(3) "*And because &c.*"—This is added in order to show why the lower forms of Dispassion cannot be the cause of Unconscious Meditation. As a rule, the cause is of the same nature as the effect ; hence we cannot postulate the *material* Dispassion as a cause of the *immaterial* meditation, which can be due only to the immaterial effulgence of wisdom. Therefore the cause of the *Immaterial* Abstract Meditation, is "the cloud of virtue" Meditation, which owes its existence to pure Goodness following on the complete destruction of the impurities of Foulness and Darkness,—and which also is Immaterial on account of the rejection of all material objects, and as such rests in itself.

(4) "*As if non-existing*"—because of the absence of its effects, the various functions.

(5) "*Seedless*"—*i.e.* beyond the range of the seeds, the troubles, the actions and the desires. This is the literal meaning, as given by Vachaspati Misra ; the real meaning being that given in the translation.

This (meditation) is of two kinds—The *Bhavapratyaya* (caused by the world) and the *Upáyápratyaya* (caused by the means). Of these the latter belongs to the Yogis.

Sutra(19):—The *world-caused* belongs to the Disembodied and to the Resolved-into-Nature.

Com. :—To the Disembodied—*i. e.* the celestial beings—belongs the World-caused (*Bhavapratyaya*). These (beings),—experiencing isolation as it were, by means of their internal organs aided by their residua alone,—carry over the residual fructifications which are cognate therewith. Similarly the Resolved-into-Nature experience isolation as it were, on the dissolution into Nature of the internal organ in its full activity; (and this experience continues only) so long as the internal organ, by its inherent authority does not return (to its work).

Notes: (1) "*Caused by the means*" *i.e.* by the means prescribed in the *S'ástras*

(2) "*Disembodied*"—Thus described by Váchaspati Misra: 'Thinking either one of the elements or one of the senses to be their spirit, contemplating on these, and hence having their internal organs coloured by a desire for these, and consequently on death, dissolving either into the senses or the (subtle Elements), their internal organs consisting only of the Residua, and finally devoid of the six-sheathed (material) body'.

(3) "*Experiencing isolation as it were by means &c.*"—the similarity between isolation and the state of the internal organ of the Disembodied depends only on the fact of the latter being devoid of its functions; the dissimilarities consisting in the fact of the internal organ being in activity and bearing a balance of the former residua.

(4) "*Carry over Etc.*"—*i. e.* are born again.

(5) "*In full activity*"—*i. e.* having its ends un-fulfilled. The ends of the internal organ would be fulfilled only on the accomplishment of discriminative knowledge.

Sutra (20):—Of others, preceded by faith, energy, memory, meditation and discrimination.

Com.:—To the *yogis* belongs the *Means-caused* (*Upáyapratyaya*). "Faith," confidence of the mind like the loving mother, sustains the *Yogi*. "Energy" accrues to an agent endued with faith and desirous of discrimination; and on the energetic attends "Memory"; on this the mind rests peacefully in contemplation; and to one of calm mind comes Discrimination; by means of which he comes to recognise things in their true colours. By constant practice of this, and by means of Dispassion with regard thereto, is brought about Unconscious or Abstract Meditation.

Notes (1) "*Faith*" *&c.*—Confidence in the senses &c are not faith because it is based on illusion, hence it is specified "*of the mind*".

(2) "*Sustains*"—*i. e.* keeps him from erring paths and keeps him fixed to the one true path of salvation.

(3) "*Memory*"—is explained by Vachaspati Misra as '*Dhyàna*' (contemplation).

(4) "*Rests &c*"—this also implies the various stages of Meditation Restraint and the rest to be described hereafter.

(5) "*Discrimination*"—so far we have the ingredients of concrete meditation. The meditation following this is Abstract meditation.

(6) "*Is brought about &c.*"—suppression following on the discriminative knowledge of the Spirit puts a stop to the activity of the internal organ, whose ends have been all fulfilled by that time.

The nine *yogis* are such as have their means mild, moderate and excessive. E. G. (1) One of mild means, (2) Of moderate means, and (3) Of excessive means; of these again the first is of three kinds: (1) The mildly—dispassionate, (2) the moderately—dispassionate and (3) the ardently—dispassionate. There are similar divisions of the moderate—means and the excessive—means.

From among these, for those of excessive means (is laid down).—

Sutra (21):—the ardently—dispassionate, proximate,

Com:—is the accomplishment of meditation, as well as its end.

Notes: (1)—"*Mild means &c.*"—These "means" are Faith and the rest just described.

(2)" *Mildly dispassionate*"—Vachaspati Misra explains "*Samvega*" as *Vairagya*" . 'Dispassion '—Though Bhojadeva and Vijnana Bhikshu both explain it as "energetic exertion" or "impetuosity"—The mildness or the excessiveness of these is due to prenatal causes.

(3) "*Its end*"—The abstract meditation as the effect of concrete meditation, and Isolation as that of the former.

Sutra (22) :—A further distinction, on acconnt of the mild, the moderate and the excessive.

Com :—There is a distinction further than this, such as: (1) The midly—ardent, (2) the moderately—ardent, and (3) the excessively—ardent. On account of this distinction, the accomplishment of meditation and its ends, is near to one of excessive means when mildly-ardently-dispassionate, nearer to him when moderately-ardently-dispassionate, and nearest to him when excessively-ardently-dispassionate.

Question:—"Is the extreme proximity of meditation due to this (above mentioned) cause alone? or is there any other means to its attainment ?"

Answer :—

Sutra (23) :—Or by devotion to God.

Com:—The Supreme God, being attracted by the devotion (of the *yogi*) favours him by mere prescience. And from this prescience also accrues to the agent, the accomplishment of meditation and its ends.

Notes: (1) "*Attracted*"—brought face to face.

(2) "*Prescience*" in the form :—" May the devoted agent attain to his desired end"—Such is the form of the prescient favour as explained by Vachaspati Misra.

(3) "*Mere prescience*"—That is by His sheer will without any form of exertion.

Question :—" Who is this God, distinct from Nature and Spirit ?"

Answer:—

***Sutra* (24) :—God is a distinct spirit, untouched by afflictions, actions, deserts and impressions.**

Com : "Afflictions,"–Ignorance and the rest. "Actions," good and evil,—the effects of these are the "Deserts,"—and desires in accordance with these, are the "Impressions"; though these reside in the internal organ, yet they are attributed to the Spirit, who is the experiencer of their results; just as defeat or victory really belonging to the soldiers, is attributed to their leader. That particular Spirit, who is untouched by such experience, is God.

Though there are many master-adepts who have attained to Isolation,—(yet) such have attained to Isolation after having cut off the three bondages ; whereas the connection of God with these has neither been nor ever will be. We do not know of any preceding bondage of God, as we do of the emancipated; nor is any future bondage possible for God, as it is for the Resolved-in-nature. He is ever Isolated and ever Supreme.

(*Question*): "This eternal supremacy of God, due to supreme goodness,—has it any proof, or is it incapable of proof ?"

(*Answer*) : Its proof lies in the Scripture.

(*Question*) : What is the proof for this Scripture ?

(*Answer*) : It lies in its supreme goodness. The connection between these two,—Scripture and its supreme character, resident as they are in God's Buddhi,—is eternal. From Scripture, it comes to this : that God is ever the Lord and ever emancipated.

And this supremacy of His is free from equality or excess, because it is never exceeded by any other supremacy ; whatever should exceed it, would become *that* itself. Hence wherever there is the final stage of supremacy, that is God.

Nor is there any supremacy equal to it. Because when there are two things equally supreme (contending) with regard to a desired object, (one saying) "may this be new" and (the other contending) "may this be old"—then (in such a case) only one can be fulfilled, and as such there would result the resistence of the will of another, which would imply the lesser character of his supremacy. And further, to two equal persons cannot belong the simultaneous accomplishment of the desired object, —the objects being contradictory. Therefore He whose supremacy is free from equality and excess, is God; and He is a distinct Spirit.

(Notes: (1) "*Though there are many master-adepts &c.*"—The objection here met is based on the following Sutras of Kapila,—I, 92, V, 1—12. (Vide Rajendralal Mitra's *Yoga Sutras*).

(2) "*The three bondages*"—(1) The natural bondage of the Resolved-in nature, (2) The modificatory bondage of the Disembodied, and (3) The Right-hand bondage of the celestials.

(3) "*Lies in supreme goodness*"—The Lord has recourse to supreme goodness for the following reasons: God has no possessive relation with the goodness of the internal organ which is due to Ignorance; He only desires to save the three-fold-bound spirits from the cycle of death, by instructions with regard to wisdom and virtue; but such instructions are not possible without the assistance of wisdom and action, which latter is not possible without having recourse to Goodness washed clear of all taint of Foulness and Darkness. This is the purity that is implied by the epithet "supreme" (*Prakrishta*).

One is said to be subject to Ignorance when he does not recognise it as such. One however who recognises Ignorance *as ignorance* and governs his actions accordingly, cannot be said to be *subject to ignorance*.

(4) "*Eternal Supremacy*"—This epithet is added to meet the objection of mutual subserviency; which is said to be no fault, when in connection with two Eternal Entities.

(5) "*What is the proof for this scripture?*"—Perceiving the infallibility of the *MantraSâstra* and the medical science, we must acknowledge the force of God's intellect, clear of all taint of Foulness and Darkness, as shining everywhere. Similarly the Scripture, consisting of instructions for the highest bliss, and owing its compilation to God, must be attributed to the excellence of his Goodness. And when Goodness reigns supreme, there is no room for doubt and deception. Thus then the validity of the scripture is based upon the excellence and supremacy of Goodness. (*cf. Nyayasutra*—II—i—53 Et. Seq.)

(6) "*The connection between these two &c.*"—This meets the objection that the Scripture, being an effect of excellence and as such leading to the inference

thereof, becomes a form of inference, and not Testimony. The reply means, that the Scripture indicates excellence, not by its character of an effect, but by means of the eternal relation of the denoter and the denoted. That is to say the excellence resides in God's Buddhi, and the Scripture too, being denotative of it, resides therein.

(7) "*It comes to this*"—Scripture, implying the excellence of God's Buddhi leads to the following conclusion.

And further,—

Sutra (25):—In Him is the highest limit of the seed of omni-science.

Com:—The seed of omniscience is the cognition of the parvitude (or smallness) and magnitude (or largeness) of the perception of supersensorious objects, past, present and future, individually as well as collectively. And that person is omniscient in whom this seed has grown to its utmost extent. There is a gradual progress of the seed of omniscience because it has various degrees, like Dimension (*parimána*). That person in whom wisdom attains its limit, is omniscient; and this is a particular Spirit.

The above inference, ending in only a general conclusion, is not capable of denoting any particular being; consequently the knowledge of particular names is to be looked for in the Scripture.

For God, though there is no selfish motive, yet there is the motive of mercy for the creatures,—(being of the form) " By means of instructions in wisdom and virtue, I shall rescue all transmigratory spirits, at the periodical and the final dissolution". As is declared: "The first Knower, Lord and Great Sage, with a view to creation, in his mercy, taught the Science to the enquiring Asuri ".

Notes: (1) "*The above inference &c.*":—This assertion precludes the possiblity of the name 'God' being applied to the various masters of the various philosophies—*e. g.* Buddha &c.

(2) "*Particular names*":—Such as Siva, Sakti &c.

(3) "*As is declared &c.*":—by Panchasikha. The " Great Sage " is Kapila an incarnation of Vishnu.

And such a one is—

Sutra (26):—the Greatest of even the earliest ones, because unconditioned by time.

Com:—The early great ones are all conditioned by time One, for whom time does not appear as a condition, is the instructor and hence the greatest of even the earlier ones; and as (the existence of such a one) is established, in this cycle, by superiority, so should it be understood with reference to the past cycles also.

Notes: (1) "*The early great ones*":—*e. g.* Brahmâ, Vishnu &c.

The aphorism serves to distinguish the supreme God from His earliest manifestations, Brahmá, Vishnu and others.

Sutra (27).—His indicator is the *Pranava*.

Com:—God is the indicated of the *Pranava*.

(*Question*): 'Is denotation of it based on convention, or is it inherent in it, like the light of the lamp' ?

(*Reply*): 'The relation of this indicated (the God) with the indicator (the *pranava*) is inherent. Convention due to God only represents objects, already existing ; as for example, the natural relation of the father and son is expressed by convention as "This is the father, and that his son." In other cycles also, convention is always dependent upon the (inherent) faculties of the indicator and the indicated. The masters of scripture declare the relation of word and meaning to be eternal because of the eternal character of universal agreement (in convention.)

Notes: (1) "*In other cycles too etc*"—This is added in anticipation of the following objection: 'Word being an effect of Nature, is resolved together with its power into its cause, on Dissolution ; consequently when the Great Principle &c., would be produced again in due course, there could be no previous *power* on which the new nomenclature would be based." The reply means to say that though the word with its *power* has once become resolved into its cause, yet when the word is again brought forth, the *power* inherent in it comes along with it. And it is in accordance with the previous relation of the word and its denotation, that God lays down the conventional names for the new cycle.

(2) "*Agreement*"—with regard to long standing usage.

For the yogi who has recognised the character of the indicator and the indicated—

Sutra (28) its repetition, and the contemplation of its meaning.

Com : The repetition of the *Pranava* and the contemplation of its denotation—God. In its manner then the internal organ of the yogi, who repeats the *pranava* and reflects on its meaning, becomes concentrated ; as is declared : "After repetition, one should have recourse to meditation ; and after meditation, again he should take to repetition. Through perfection in repetition and meditation the supreme spirit lightens" (*Vishnu Purana-*)

Notes : (1) "*Becomes concentrated*"—and then follows the direct perception of the supreme spirit; and hence the higher dispassion, and finally, Abstract meditation.

(2) "*After repetition*" of the *pranava*.

What more accrues to him ?

Sutra (29) :—Hence the cognition of "reversed perception" and absence of obstacles.

Com :—All the obstacles—disease and the rest—cease to exist, by virtue of devotion to God. And to him belongs the perception of his real character. "As God is a Spirit, pure, blissful, isolated and free from troubles,—so also is this spirit, the counter-cogniser of Buddhi (intellect) "—such being the recognition.

Notes :—(1) "*Reversed perception &c.*"—Vachaspati Misra explains this as *the Spirit subject to illusion* ; and interprets the aphorism thus : Thence accrues to him the cognition of the real character of the spirit of contradictory perception (*i. e.* the spirit under illusion). And this is quite in keeping with the *Bhashya* which explains as "*Swarupadarsanamapyasya bhavati* " (" to him accrues the perception of his real character "). The interpretation of the Bhojavritti is very subtle, very inviting; and I quote the explanatory note of Dr. Rajendralal Mitra: "The natural function of the senses is to extend out, wards in order to receive the impressions of external objects and carry them to the sensorium, but that being suppressed by the Yogi, the senses turn inwards and find their object within, and therefore the function is called 'reversed' or reflex. The object of this roundabout way of description is to say that the senses hold communion exclusively with the soul." The final upshot of both the interpretations is the same, the only difference lying in the interpretation of the epithet *pratyak*, the Vachaspatya making it—contradictory

knower (subject to illusion); and the Bhojavritti, explaining it as "turned back" (inwards instead of outwards). Hence the words "reversed perception" have been placed within inverted commas in the *Sutra*—thus admitting of both interpretations.

(2) "*Real character*"—i. e. spiritual character.

(3) "*Pure*"—i. e. unchanging and hence free from rise and fall.

(4) "*Isolated*"—Free from the effects of virtue and vice.

(5) "*Troubles*"—Birth, life and experience.

(6) "*Counter-cogniser of the intellect*"—Though the supreme spirit and the spirit in general are both similar, yet there is some difference in similarity, and this epithet serves to point out that dissimlarity.

The contemplation of one object leads to a cognition of its similars. So by the contemplation of one's human spirit, there arises the re-cognition of the supreme spirit.

Question : Which are the obstacles, and what the agitations of the internal organ; and how many are they?

Sutra (30):—Disease, Languor, Doubt, Carelessness, Sloth, Worldly-mindedness, Mistaken Notions, Missing the Point, and Instability;—these causing the distraction of the internal organ are the obstacles.

Com:—The obstacles, the distractors of the internal organ are nine. These are possible only in the company of the functions of the internal organ, which latter too are not possible without these. "Disease"—disorder of the humours, fluids and the senses. "Languor"—incapability of the internal organ to work. "Doubt"—cognition touching both ends of a subject—'this may be, this may not be'. "Carelessness" —non-reflection on the means of meditation. "Sloth"—Inactivity of the body and mind, due to lethargy. "Worldly-mindedness"—desire with regard to the connection of the internal organ with sensorious objects. "Mistaken Notions"—contrary or false cognition. "Missing the Point"—non-acquirement of the state of meditation. "Instability"—the unfixed character of the internal organ with regard to the stages already acquired. The mind would become steady for the accomplishment of meditation.

These are the distractors of the internal organ, the nine impurities of meditation, also called the "Enemies" and "obstacles" of meditation.

Sutra (31):—Pain, Irritation, Trembling, Inspirationand Expiration are the companions of distractions.

Com:—"Pain"—the natural, the terrestrial and the cellestial Pain is that, being struck by which living beings try for its exterpation. "Irritation"—agitation of the mind, due to non-fulfilment of desire. "*Trembling*"—that which shakes the body. "Inspiration"—is that breath which touches (draws) the external air; and "Expiration" is that which expels the internal air.

These are the companions of distractions. These happen to those whose minds are distracted; and not to those whose minds are at peace.

Notes:—(1) "*Pain*"—The "natural" pains are the diseases of the body and the like; "terrestrial pains" are those that are due to earthly beings, such as serpents, tigers &c; and "celestial pains" are such as are due to the influences of planets and the like.

(2) "*Trembling*"—Disturbs the posture, and thence the mind.

(3) "*Inspiration*"—Disturbs the '*Rêchaka*' and "expiration the" *Pûraka*.

Sutra (32):—For their prevention, exercise on one principle.

Com:—One ought to apply the internal organ fixed upon one single principle, for the prevention of distraction. One whose internal organ consists in mere cognition based upon several objects, and transitory, such a one's internal organ can never be concentrated, and as such must be distracted. If however it is drawn away from all other objects, and fixed on any one object, then it becomes concentrated, and hence not based on several objects.

One who thinks the internal organ to be concentrated when it is found to consist in an uninterrupted flow of similar cognitions,—for him, if concentration is a property of the current of the internal organ, then (there is the objection that) such a current cannot be *one*, because it is momentary. If however the concentration be said to belong to the cognition, only so far as the current is concerned,—then (there is the objection that in that case, the whole of this (current), consisting either in the current of *similar* cognitions, or of dissimilar ones, would be fixed upon several objects, and as such concentrated ; and as such there could never be any distraction of the internal organ. Therefore it must be concluded that the internal organ is one, and has many objects. Again if by the *one* internal organ were brought about unconnected and heterogenous (or dissimilar) cognitions then, one cognition would remember the object perceived by another cognition, and one would experience the effects of the karmic residua gathered by another cognition. Such a cognition, even if in any way fixed, would imply the rule of "the cowdung and milk-pudding."

And further, if the internal organ were different, then the (Bauddha would fall into the danger of) having done away with the cognition of his self. How ? "I am touching what I had seen," "I am seeing what I had touched "—such a cognition is present to the agent as being identical, though the cognitions themselves are different. How would this consciousness of a single cognition, the cognition of the identical self,—existing in several and altogether dissimliar internal organs—rest itself upon a single conscious agent ? This consciousness of personal identity is quite perceptible to the agent ; and certainly the force of perception is not affected by any other proof ; for all other proofs owe their strength in usage to perception alone.

Therefore the internal organ is one, fixed upon various objects, and is steady.

Notes:—" *One principle* "—*i. e.* God.

(2) " *Based upon several objects*"—That is beginning and ending in the semblance of the objects themselves, be these one or many, and not extending to others.

(3) " *Transitory* "—This epithet is added in order to preclude the possibility of the internal organ perceiving another object after having perceived one

object already. A momentary organ can never perceive more than one object. In the yoga system however the internal organ not being momentary is capable of running over many objects in a single moment; and as such it is subject to distraction.

(4) "*One who thinks &c.*"—The opinion of a section of the nihilists who hold that though no distraction is possible in a single momentary internal organ, it would be possible in an everlasting current of the internal organ.

(5) "*Such a current cannot be one*"—That is one and connected with many cognitions, as they happen to come forth. Such a one cannot be momentary; and anything other than this, the nihilist denies.

(6) "*The cowdung and the pudding*"—*i. e.* the vulgar reasoning that the cowdung is the pudding, because both owe their existence to the cow.

Question. For some, this system lays down the "purifier". Whence is this?

Sutra (33):—The peacefulness of the internal organ through friendliness, compassion, complacency and indifference in regard to pleasure and pain, and virtue and vice.

Com:—One ought to bear friendship towards all the beings that may be enjoying pleasure; compassion towards the distressed; complacency towards the virtuous; and indifference towards the vicious. To one who thus bears himself, accrues pure virtue; thence the internal organ becomes cheerful (peaceful); and being cheerful, it becomes concentrated, and attains to steadiness.

Notes:—(1) "*For some*"—*i. e.* The internal organ for which the purifications are laid down.

(2) "*Friendliness*"—Removes envy.

(3) "*Compassion*"—The thought of removing another's pain removes the sinful desire of harming others.

(4) "*Complacency*"—Towards the virtuous, removes envy.

(5) "*Indifference*"—Removes anger.

(6) "*Pure virtue*"—*i. e.* Abounding in goodness.

Sutra (34):—Or by expulsion and retention of breath.

Com:—The throwing out of the internal air through the nostrils, by a special effort, is "Expulsion;" 'Retention' is the regulation of breath. By these two means also is one to bring about steadiness of the internal organ.

Sutra (35):—Or Cognition resulting from sensuous objects may be the cause of steadiness.

Com:—Of one who concentrates (his mind) on the tip of the nose, the consciousness of superphisical odour is the disposition of smell; by concentration on the tip of the tongue, the consciousness of taste; that of colour, in the palate; that of touch, in the centre of the tongue; and that of sound at the base of the tongue. These dispositions, when produced, bind the internal organ to steadiness, remove all doubt, and become the means of meditative wisdom. A similar objective cognition is to be understood with regard to the cognitions of the sun, the moon, the planets, the gems and the like.

Though all principles, got at through the various sciences, inferences and the instructions of teachers, are always true,—because all these agents have the capacity of expounding only true principles,—yet, so long as even a single portion thereof has not been amenable to one's own sense-organs, the whole of it appears far removed, and as such does not bring about the steadiness of the internal organ with regard to such subtle entities, as Isolation and the like. Therefore for the sake of strengthening the scientific, inferential and tutorial doctrines, one should always try to directly perceive any one of the particulars. And when a particular portion of the imparted doctrine has been directly perceived, then the agent gains faith in even the subtlest elements thereof, ending in Isolation. For this reason is this (objective congnition) called "the perfection or embellishment of the internal organ."

With regard to the non-fixed (*i. e.* stray) cognitions, when there has been produced the *Consciousness of having subdued* (*Vasîkârasanjnâ*) with regard thereto, then would it (the internal organ) be capable of directly perceiving the various objects. And on this will follow unimpeded, faith, energy, memory and meditation.

Sutra (36):—Or the sorrowless, luminous.—

Com:—Add "disposition when produced causes the steadiness of the internal organ"—this much has to be continued (from the last aphorism). The perception (or consciousness) of the internal organ belonging to one who fixes on the lotus of the heart, is of two kinds: (1) The "sorrowless", the objective, and (2) the pure egotism or self-consciousness which latter disposition is also called the "luminous"; whereby the internal organ of the *yogi* attains to steadiness. The internal organ in its goodness is effulgent and like the sky; and the disposition due to the purity of steadiness therein, develops into the form of the brightness of the sun, the moon, the planets and the precious gems. Similarly, the internal organ, fallen upon egotism or self-consciousness, becomes similar to the still waters of the ocean, calm and endless; in connection herewith is declared; "(The agent), having thought of the atomic self, has the notion of, *I am*."

Notes:—(1) "*Sorrowless*,"—without pain.

(2) "*Lotus of the heart*"—There is a lotus, between the stomach and sternum, with its face downwards; the *yogi* has to turn it upwards by means of the *Rechaka*, and concentrate his mind upon it. Within the lotus the *Sushumnâ nâdi* has its rise; and since this *Nâdi* is the place assigned to the internal organ, therefore by fixing upon this lotus, the *yogi* attains to consciousness of the internal organ.

(3) "*Like the Sky*"—That is, extending everywhere.

(4) "*Similarly &c.*"—Having explained the condition of the internal organ (which is an effect of egotism) the commentator now explains that egotism itself.

(5) "*Calm*"—*i. e.* devoid of the waves of Rajas and Tamas.

(6) "*Pure egotism*"—Not like many brightnesses, spoken of with reference to the preceding.

(7) "*As is declared*"—By Panchasikha.

Sutra (37)—Or the internal organ having for its object the passionless.

Com:—The internal organ of the *yogi*, coloured by its object, and the internal organ of persons devoid of attachment, attain to steadiness.

Notes:—(1) "*Attachment*"—*i. e.* Longings for the objects of sense.

Sutra (38)—Or that depending on knowledge resulting from dream or sleep.

Com:—The *Yogi's* internal organ, depending on the knowledge in dreams, or that in sleep, and becoming of the same form as these, attains to steadiness.

Notes:—(1) "*Sleep*"—*i. e.*, one abounding in *Sattva*.

(The knowledge referred to in the *Sutra* is such as the vision in a dream of the particular form of a particular God and so on).

Sutra (39):—Or by meditating according to one's predilection.

Com:—One ought to meditate upon the object which is most to his liking. The internal organ, having acquired steadiness in that, will be able to attain to it elsewhere also.

Notes:—(1) "*The object and &c.*"—That is the form of any particular God or Goddess which best suits the agent's fancy.

Sutra (40):—His mastery extends from the minutest atom to infinite magnitude.

Com:—By thinking (or applying the mind) on minute

objects (the *Yogi*) acquires steadiness (with regard to objects up to the minutest atom; and by thinking on the gross objects he attains to the steadiness of the internal organ, extending to the utmost limit of infinity. Thus then (to the *Yogi*) who runs over both these ends, belongs non-bafflement (or non-disturbance); and this is supreme "Mastery." The internal organ of the *Yogi*, having become accomplished through this mastery, no longer stands in need of the purifications brought about by practice (or exercise).

Notes:—(1) Now—What are the form and the object of the consciousness of the internal organ, which has attained to steadiness? This is described in the next Sutra.

Sutra (41):—To him of over-powered functions, like that of a clear gem, there is,—with regard to the cogniser, the means of cognition, and the cognised —the modification, consciousness or state of similarity, identity, or cosubstantiation with these, of that which rests in them.

Com:—"*To him of over-powered functions*"—To one whose cogitations have been suppressed. "Like that of a clear gem" only cites an example. As a rock-crystal, affected by the forms of the several objects (presented to it), appears similar to them; so the internal organ, being affected by its object, the "cognised," and thereby assuming its character, appears in the same form. That which is affected by minute elements, assumes their character, and as such appears in the same form; similarly that which is affected by a gross object, assumes its character and hence appears in a gross form; and lastly, in the same manner, that which is affected by the various modifications of the universe, assumes the character of such modifications, and as such appears in the same form. In the same manner, we should find with regard to the "Means of cognition," *i.e.* the sense-organs. (The internal organ) affected by the sense-organs, assumes their character and as such appears in the form. Similarly, when it is affected by the cognising agent as its object, it acquires his character and as such appears form; and in the same manner becoming affected by the Free Spirit, it becomes identical therewith, and hence appears in that form.

Such is the character of the internal organ, similar to that of transparent jewels, consisting in its identity, on cosubstantiation,—in matters relating to the cogniser, the means of cognition and the cognised, *i. e.* to the spirit, the sense-organs and the elements,—with these (cogniser &c.), of that which rests in them (in this case the internal organ itself). And this is called the *Samapáti* (condition, modification or consciousness).

Notes:—(1) "*Of over-powered functions*"—*i. e.* free from all taint of *Tamas* and *Rajas*.

(2) "*Minute objects*"—This includes all entities, from Nature down to the rudimentary elements.

(3) "*Modifications of the Universe*"—All objects, animate or inanimate.

***Sutra* (42) :—The argumentative condition is that which is mixed with the modification of words, meaning and understanding (or idea.)**

Com:—As for example, we find that with regard to the three aspects—'cow' the word, 'cow' the meaning or object, and 'cow' the knowledge or idea—we have an undifferentiated or joint perception, though the three are really distinct from one another. Where however, they are differentiated, there are some properties of the word, others of the meaning, and others again of the idea,—Such is the way of their differentiation. If the object 'cow', rising to the contemplative consciousness of the *yogi* engaged in the aforesaid (fanciful perception), happens to be affected by the modification of word, meaning and idea, then it becomes of a mixed up condition, and is called the "argumentative."

Note:—(1) We fancy the identity of the object 'cow' and the word when pointing to the animal as a 'cow', and this identity is further transferred to the idea of the animal in the mind of the speaker and the listener.

When on the other hand, in the contemplative consciousness, which is free from all notions of verbal convention as well as from all modification of knowledge due to valid testimony and inference,—then there appears the object in its own real form, characterised by nothing but this form alone; and that condition is the "Non-argumentative." This is the highest perception; and it is the root of valid testimony and inference, both of these arising from it. Such a perception cannot be said to occur in the company of knowledge due to assertion and inference. Therefore the perception of the *yogi* due to non-argumentative Meditation, is unmixed with any other kind of right notion: and the author explains the definition of this non-argumentative condition, by means of the following aphorism:—

Sutra (43):—The non-argumentative is that in which, on the dissolution of memory, the meaning (or object,) alone, is apparent, and which appears as if devoid of its own identity.

Com.:—All verbal convention, fancy with regard to knowledge due to testimony and inference, and memory, having been dissolved,—the consciousness, coloured by the form of the object of cognition (*acceptance*), forsakes, as it were, that form of its own which is constituted by the *acceptance*) or cognition, and becomes solely of the form of the *object* —*i. e.* assumes the form of the *object* of (acceptance or) cognition; and this (consciousness) is the non-argumentative condition. Thus has this been explained already (in the prefatory remarks to this aphorism).

The object of this condition is the universe of objects, animate or inanimate, which consists (respectively) in the object as a whole (in the case of animate objects) or in a particular agglomeration of minute particles (in the case of inanimate objects), and which gives rise to a unitary consciousness (*i. e.* the consciousness of the object as a single whole). This particular agglomeration (the gross object,) is the common property of the minute particles (constituting it); and as such constituting their very nature, it is inferred from the manifested effect (the notion of the object as a whole), and presents itself, through agencies leading to its manifestation; and disappears on the appearance of other properties (of the same particles). This same property (described above) is called the "component" (whole), which is 'one, large, small, tangible, active, and transient'; it is by means of such component wholes that all business is carried on. One to whom such a particular agglomeration is nothing (and the object of abstract perception), and whom a minute (or subtle) cause is imperceptible (even to abstract undeterminate perception),—to such a one, there being no component whole, all knowledge would be false—false knowledge having been defined as "notion abiding in a form which is not that of the object" (aph. 7). And under the circumstances there being no object, what could be his true knowledge? Whatever object is perceived has been decided to be a component whole. Therefore it must be admitted that there is a component whole, bearing the usage of largeness &c., which becomes the object of the non-argumentative condition.

Notes :—(1) "*Which gives rise to unitary consciousness*"—*i. e.* the notion of the perceived object as one complete whole in itself.

(2) "*This particular agglomeration &c.*"—The object as a whole is the common property of each and every one of the particles constituting it and not of any one set of them. That is to say each constituting atom has in itself the miniature, so to say, of the object as a whole.

(3) "*Which consists respectively in the object as a whole &c.*" the epithet "giving rise to a unitary consciousness" is directed against the Vaibhashika view of every object being only an agglomeration of particles, which denies the existence of any object as a complete whole in itself. The epithet "which consists in the object as a whole" is directed against the Yogachara idealistic view that nothing exists save the 'idea.' And lastly the epithet "which consists in a particular agglomeration of particles" is directed against the atomic theory of the Vaishesikas.

(4) "*Inferred from the manifested effect*"—It may be here noted that the Bhashya here is driving at the "Effect—an—Entity" theory of the Sankhya philosophy; in asmuch as the atom is said to carry in itself the miniature of its effect, the object constituted by it.

(5) "*On the appearance of other properties*"—*i. e.* When the particles have the property of the 'jar' then there is the jar; when however any foreign cause produces in the same particles the property of 'Kapala' (a piece of the jar) then the former object, the jar, disappears.

(6) "*One to whom such &c.*"—According to the Bauddhas the agglomeration of the particles though insignificant is yet perceptible to the indeterminate or abstract perception; whereas the subtile cause is not perceptible even to such a perception. Vachaspati misra reads—"*Yasya punaravastukah prachayavisashahé*"; and this reading has been followed in the translation.

Sutra (44) :—**By this, the deliberative and the non-deliberative, as pertaining to subtile objects, are also described.**

Com :—Of these that condition is called the 'deliberative' which pertains to the subtile Elements, whose properties have been manifested, and which are characterised by a notion of their place, time and cause. Of this also that which appears as the object of Meditative consciousness is such a subtile element as is qualified by an apparent property, and amenable to Unitary consciousness (*see above*). On the other hand, the "non-deliberative" condition is that which appertains in all ways and by all means to such subtile objects as are free from the specialisation of all properties past, present, and future, and yet accompanied by all properties, and containing them. Being of such character, the subtile Element by means of this same form becomes an object (of perception), and as such colours (or affects) the form of meditative consciousness. When this consciousness loses its own identity (form) and consists solely in the object, it is called the "non-deliberative." Of these the "argumentative" and the "non-argumentative" appertain to gross (extended) objects, whereas the "deliberative" and the "non-deliberative" appertain to the subtile ones. Thus also by this very "non-argumentative" (condition) has been described the destruction of fancy with regard to both.

Notes:—(1) "*A notion of place, time and cause*"—The causal series is thus laid down: the Earth-atom from the five rudimentary Elements abounding in the odoriferous Element, and so on.

(2) "*Of this that which appears &c.*"—This points out the similarity between the "deliberative" and the "argumentative" of the last aphorisom.

(3) "*In all ways by all means &c.*"—That is, *in* all the forms of red, green, yellow &c. and *by* the notions of place, time and cause. This implies that the atoms are not affected by the limitations of time,—not even through the properties begun in time as is implied by the Epithet "*Sântodita.*" But for all this, the atom is related to the properties ("*Sarvadharmànupàtishu*") as being their substratum.

(4) "*Fancy with regard to both*"—The fancy of word and meaning with regard to the "non-deliberative" and the "non-argumentative;" and *not* the "deliberative and the non-deliberative" as Vijnana Bhikshu explains; because the deliberative is free from the aforesaid fancy.

Sutra (45):—The Subtile objectivity terminates in the indissoluble.

Com:—Of the Earth—atom the odoriferous Element is the subtile object; of the Aqueous, the taste-Element; of the Fiery, the colour—Element; of the Aerial, the tactile Element;

of Space (*ákâsa*), the sound-Element; of these (the rudimentary Elements), again, self-consciousness is the subtile object; of self-consciousness, the "dissoluble" (Buddhi); of this Buddhi too the subtile object is the "Indissoluble" (Nature). And there is no subtile entity beyond the "Indissoluble." If it be urged that—"The Spirit is such a subtile entity,"—we reply—true; the subtility of the Spirit (with regard to Nature) is not of the same character as that of Nature over Buddhi. "What is it then?" Spirit is not the *material* cause of the "dissoluble," though it is an *instrumental* cause. Therefore the subtilest of the subtile terminates in Nature.

Notes: (1) "*Not the material causes*"—The series of comparative subtility is based on the fact of the subtiler being the material cause of the immediate grosser object, and is as much as Spirit is not the material cause of anything, its subtility is of quite a different order, not to be considered here.

Sutra (46):—These verily constitute "seeded" meditation.

Com:—These four conditions have external objects for their seed; consequently the meditation is seeded. Among these, that with regard to gross objects, is "argumentative" and "non-argumentative," and that with regard to subtile objects, is "deliberative" and "non-deliberative,"—thus four-fold has meditation been numbered.

Sutra (47):—On the purity of the non-deliberative, internal perspicuity.

Com:—"Purity" consists in the steady current—untainted by *Tamas* and *Rajas* and hence clear of the principle of spiritual consciousness, consisting in brightness (or illumination) and free from the touch of all masking impurities. When this purity accrues to non-deliberative meditation, then to the *yogi* belongs "internal perspicuity,"—*i. e.* a clear conscious vision, irrespective of all sequence, with regard to real objects; as is declared: "The wise reaching to the perspicuity of consciousness, look upon all beings, as a man on a mountain top does upon those on the ground below,—thinking of (other) beings, while being himself unthinkable."

Notes: (1) *"Irrespective of sequence."*—*i. e.* Simultaneous, perceiving all objects at one stroke.

Sutra (48):—Therein consciousness is truth-bearing.

Com:—During the aforesaid condition, the consciousness of the meditative one, has the name of "truth-bearing;" and this name is applicable literally; because such consciousness supports truth alone, there being not a trace of untruth; as is declared; "By valid testimony, by inference, and by a respectful exercise of contemplation, bringing about his consciousness, one attains to supreme union (*yoga*)."

And this again—

Sutra (49):—has its subject different from those of revealed and inferential consciousness, because it refers to particulars.

Com:—"Revealed"—the knowledge due to the scriptures; this refers to generals; for certainly the scripture can never denote particulars. Why? Because, the word (on which revelation is based) has not its usage based on particulars. Similarly inference also refers to generals alone? (The typical form of inference being)—where approach is, there is access, and where there is non-approach, there is no access. Inference leads to conclusions only by generalities. Therefore there can be no particularity which can be the object of either revelation or inference. Nor is this subtile, veiled (occult) and magnificent object (of meditation) amenable to ordinary perception. Nor, lastly, can we deny the existence of such a particular, as unproved. Therefore this particular object—whether pertaining to the subtile Elements or to Spirit—is amenable to meditative consciousness alone. Therefore the aforesaid consciousness has an object different from those of revealed and inferential consciousness, because it appertains to particulars.

Sutra (50); The impression or residum due to this is contradictory to other impressions.

Com:—The impression (residuum) arising from meditative consciousness obstructs the residuum of impression produced by the worldly condition (Vyutthana). And the impressions of the worldly condition having been suppressed, the cognitions due to these are no longer produced; and these cognitions being suppressed, meditation comes forward; then follows meditative consciousness, and in its wake, the impressions produced by that consciousness. Thus everytime a new residuum of impressions is produced giving rise to a fresh supply of consciousness, which again in its turn would bring about fresh impressions. (*Question*): "Wherefore will this excess of impressions not afford power *i. e.* function, or capacity to the internal organ"? (*Reply*): The impressions brought about by the aforesaid consciousness do not give power to the internal organ; because they are the means of the removal of pain; in fact they serve to separate the internal organ from its functionings; for the functionings of the internal organ has its termination discriminative in wisdom.

What occurs to this? (Reply):

Sutra (51):—On the suppression of this also, all being suppressed, (there is) meditation without a seed.

Com:—And this is an obstacle not only to meditative consciousness, but also to all impressions produced by this consciousness. Why? Because the impressions produced by suppression always obstruct those produced by meditation. And the existence of impressions, produced by the suppressive mind, is to be inferred from the experience of the sequence of time with regard to the suppressed state of the internal organ. The internal organ resolves itself into its own permanent Prakriti (nature,) along with all the impressions, produced by the waking, the suppressed and the meditative conditions, partaking of isolation. Therefore such impressions are obstacles to the activity of the internal organ, and as such do not lead to its continuance. And thereby the internal organ, divested of its functions, desists along with the impressions of the isolated state ;—and on the suppression of this, the Spirit abides in its own form, and hence is called *pure and liberated.*

Notes (1) " *Impressions produced by suppression* "—That is by that which suppresses the aforesaid consciousness.

SECTION II.

OF THE MEANS TO MEDITATION.

The Yoga belonging to one of pacified mind, has been expounded. Now begins the (consideration of the question); 'How would one whose mind is in the waking (worldly) state, achieve Yoga ?'

Sutra (*1*):—Asceticism, Study, and Resignation to God constitute Active a Preliminary Yoga.

Com. :—Yoga is not achieved by the non-ascetic. Asceticism is a means (to Yoga), because without asceticism it is impossible to distend the (bonds of) impurities, entangled in the meshes of sensuous objects, and intermixed with endless actions, afflictions, and desires. And the asceticism (here meant) is the undisturbed or unchecked peace of mind which is to be striven after by the yogi—such has been declared in the scriptures. "Study"—the repetition of the sacred words, as the Praṇava and the rest, or the study of the science treating of Liberation.

"*Resignation to God*"—the offering of all actions to the Supreme Teacher or venerable (God), or the relinquishment of their fruits.

Notes :—"*And asceticism &c.*"—The Commentator here distinctly denies the theory of pennance and the like religious austerities being the means to Yoga. In his opinion a peaceful equilibrium of mind alone can lead to Yoga.

"Study"—Aph. 44 of Chap. II would support the second interpretation of the Comy.

And this Active Yoga—

Sutra (2) :—Is for the contemplation of Samadhi and for the attenuation of distractions.

Com :—Active Yoga, being striven after, leads to the cognition of *Samâdhi*, and attenuates the distractions;

and the distractions, being thus attenuated, are bound to have their roots burnt up as it were by the fire of wisdom, and thus to be deprived of their productive capacity. They having been attenuated, the descriminative knowledge of the difference between the material attributes and the Spirit, being untainted by distractions, and thus constituting the subtle consciousness;—has its functions finished, and is fit for the dissolution (*literally*, retrograde progress).

Notes :—(1) " *Subtle* "—because beyond the reach of the senses. (2) " *Functions* "—The production of various effects.

Now what are the distractions, and how many are they ? (Reply) :—

Sutra (3) :—Ignorance, Egoism, Desire, Aversion, and Attachment are the five distractions.

Com :—" Distractions "— that is to say the five misconceptions (I—8). These issuing forth strengthen the *power* (capacity) of the attributes, establish the various modifications, lay open the current of cause and effect, and lastly, depending upon mutual aid, bring out the fructification of Karma.

Notes—(1) " *Mutual aid* "—Vâchaspati Mis'ra explains this as being the mutual dependence of actions and distractions, the one giving rise to the other, by turns. Vijnâna Bhiks'hu and others explain it as that between the five distractions themselves—Ignorance producing Desire, Desire Ignorance and so on.

Sutra (4) :—Ignorance is the breeding ground for those that follow—(*whether they be*) dormant, weak, intercepted, or operative.

Com :—Here " Ignorance " is the " breeding ground " *i e.*, the productive ground of the following :—*i.e.*, Egoism and the rest which are assumed to be of four kinds—dormant, weak, intercepted and operative.

Of these, what is dormancy? It is the germinal condition of the distractions abiding in the mind only by their latent potency (*i. e.*, not yet existing in reality). The awakening of these consists in their proximity to their respective objects. For one, however, who has wisdom, and the seed of whose distractions has been burnt up,—this does not exist, even, on the presentation of the object. For, whence the sprouting of a burnt seed? For this reason, the expert, whose distractions are at an end, is called the "*Charamadéha*" (Lit. The *Last-body*). It is only in such a body, and no where else, that distractions attain the fifth condition—wherein the seed has been burnt. In that condition the existing distractions have their productive faculty burnt up, and hence even on the proximity of the objects they have no awakening. Thus has been described "dormancy" as also the non-production of the burnt seeds.

"Weakness" is (now) described: Distractions become weak, by being put down by contrary practices. Similarly on being intercepted again and again, they appear again by means of their respective forms,—and are thus said to be "intercepted". How? Because anger is not seen simultaneously with attachment. For certainly anger does not operate at a time when there is attachment. And further, the fact of attachment existing with regard to one object does not lead to the inference of the absence of attachment with regard to (all) other objects. For the assertion that "Chaitra is attached to one woman" does not lead to the conclusion that "he has an aversion towards all other women"; all that is meant by the former assertion is that attachment is already *in operation* with regard to the particular woman, whereas with regard to other women it has only got a potency to become operative at some future time. And such a (distraction endued with a future potency) becomes either dormant or weak or intercepted. That which is already operating with regard to its object, is said to be "operative".

All these do not go beyond the limits of distraction. Which distraction then, is intercepted, dormant, weak or operative? This will be explained later on. True—but they have been said to be "intercepted &c." only with regard to their particular phases. As it is suppressed by contrary agencies, so it is rendered manifest by its manifesting causes.

All these distractions are forms of ignorance. Why? Because Ignorance pervades through all of them. The form that Ignorance gives to an object, by that form alone do the distractions abide; and they are found to exist simultaneously with misconception, as well as to disappear with Ignorance.

Notes: (I) "*It is only in such a body &c.*": This anticipates the question why the "burnt-seed" was not mentioned as one of the conditions of distraction. The reason given is that the condition in question is found only in the case of the wise one who is in his last body and is not going to be born again,—hence as there is no production of the distraction in this condition, Ignorance cannot be the productive soil for it.

(2) "*All these do not go beyond &c.*"—This is said in anticipation of the objection that as the "operative" ones alone are the distractors, why should the others be called "distractions" at all?

The reply is that as the others too have a latent potency of becoming operative in time, on the presentation of suitable objects, they are also included in the denotation of the word "distraction".

"*Which distraction then is &c.*"—If all are the same, wherefore the different names?

(4) "*Such a one becomes dormant &c.*"—When a certain distraction is operating, the distraction equipped with a latent future potency becomes dormant with regard to a certain object, weak with regard to another, and intercepted with regard to a third. For certainly it cannot be said to be non-existing; as in that case its appearance at any future time would be impossible.

(5) "*Intercepted*"—"Those afflictions are said to be 'intercepted' which remain with their powers overcome by a particularly potent passion, as desire when the prevailing passion is aversion, or aver-

sion when the prevailing passion is desire, being opposed to each other, they cannot dominate at the same time, (one must for the time intercept the other)"—*Bhoja* (*Mitra*).

(6) "*By its manifesting causes*"—Such as continued brooding over the distracting objects.

"*Manifested*"—*i. e.* rendered operative.

The form of Ignorance is now described :

Sutra (5) :—Ignorance is the notion of the identity of the eternal, the pure, the joyous and the spirit, with that which is non-eternal, impure, painful and non-spirit.

Com :—The cognisance of eternality in non-eternal effects *e. g.* 'the permanent earth', 'permanent the heavens together with the moon and stars', 'Immortal the celestial beings.'

Similarly there is a cognition of purity in the impure and disgusting body : it being declared : "on account of the position, the seed, the constituents and also on account of death, and lastly on account of purity being imposed upon it,—the learned have declared the body to be impure." *e. g.* "Beautiful like the fresh moon, this girl appears as if her limbs were made up of honey and ambrosia, or as if she had emerged from the moon ; and she, having eyes like the blue lotus leaves, by means of her love-ful eyes, enlivens as it were, the living world" :—(in this) what has any relation to what ? (*A.* The whole is altogether an unconnected whole). Thus we find that there is a mistaken notion of purity with regard to impure things. Similar to this is the idea of virtue in vice, and that of useful in the useless.

In the same manner, the notion of pleasure in pain will be spoken of in aphorism 15 of section II. The idea of pleasure in the pain spoken of in the aphorism referred to is Ignorance.

Similarly, the idea of spirit in the non-spirit, such as in the external accessories, sentient as well as insentient,—or in the body which is the substratum of experience,—or in the mind, the accessory of the spirit. In this connection it is declared: "Taking the manifested or unmanifested accessories to be his self, he rejoices in their prosperity, thinking such prosperity to be his own; and deplores their calamity, thinking it to be his own;—such a one is altogether deluded." (*Panchaśikhâchârya*).

Such is Ignorance, having four feet as it were, the root of all the series of troubles, as also of all karmic residua, together with their fructification. Like the words *Amitra* and *Agoshpada*, Ignorance (*Avidya*) is a positive entity. As the word 'Amitra' does not denote the *absence of a friend*, nor *a single friend*, but it denotes something contradictory thereto,—an enemy;—and again as the word *Agoshpada* does not denote the *absence of the foot-print of the cow*, nor *the single foot print of the cow*; on the other hand, it denotes something quite other than these two, —a particular country; in the same manner *Ignorance* is neither *right conception*, *nor the absence of right conception*,—it is quite an independent idea by itself, opposed to knowledge or wisdom.

Note :—(1) "*External accessories*."—Accessories related to the body—such as father, mother, child, bed, clothes &c.

(2) "*Manifested and the unmanifested &c.*"—The manifested ones are the animate accessories—parent, son, brothers; and the unmanifested ones are the bed, clothes &c., the inanimate ones.

(3) The sense of the last parapaph is that though formed of the two particles *a* (=not) and *Vidyâ* (=knowlege), the word *Avidyâ* does not mean simple *absence of knowledge* but a conception quite distinct therefrom. Just as the word *Amitra*, formed by *a* (=not) and *miera*, (=friend) does not mean either *absence of friend*, or a *single friend* (the

compound in this being broken up as *Na Mitro yasmât*), but simply something opposed to both of these, an enemy; and similarly the word *Agoshpada* formed by *a* (=not) and *goshpada* (=foot-print of a cow) does not mean what the constituent particles directly denote, but it forms the name of a country.

Sutra (6):—Egoism is the identifying of the power that sees with the power of seeing.

Com:—Spirit being the "power that sees", and the mind the "power of seeing",—the conception of the identity of these two constitutes the distinction of egoism. It is only on the non-discrimination of the two quite unblended and distinct powers of the *enjoyer* and *enjoyed* that enjoyment arises; when however, the true nature of the two has been ascertained, there follows isolation, and all enjoyment disappears. This has been thus declared: "Not perceiving the spirit, which is above mind, and which is distinct from it by reason of its form, character, wisdom and the like,—one forms of the idea of self therein (in the mind) only through stupidity"—(*Panchaśikhâchârya*.)

Notes:—"*Distinct from it &c*"—the "form" of the spirit is eternal purity as distinct from the impurity of the mind; its "character" is that of a *witness* as apart from the partial nature of the *mind*; and lastly spirit has wisdom (*i.e.*, the sentient faculty) as apart from the mind which is radically insentient.

Sutra (7):—Desire is that which dwells on pleasure.

Com:—Desire is the hankering after pleasure or its means, preceded by a rememberance of the pleasure, belonging to one who has had experience of that pleasure.

Sutra (8):—Aversion is that which dwells on pain.

Com:—Aversion consists in the anger, desire for removal, of pain or its means, preceded by a remembrance of pain,—belonging to one who has had experience of that pain.

Sutra (9).—**The well-known (distraction), that which flows in the current of its own residua, and which is well known to the learned even, is Attachment (or Tenacity of Life).**

To all living beings there is the constant selfish wish—'May I not cease to be.' 'May I continue to exist.' And such a selfish desire does not belong to one who has not experienced the experience. This is the distraction called "Attachment (to Life)," which flows in the current of its own residua. To the lowest worm just born there is a fear of death, consisting in a consciousness of its (coming) annihilation, not borne out by either perception or inference, or valid testimony;—and as such it testifies to the pangs of death experienced in previous births. As this distraction is found among the extremely stupid, so is it found to be known to the learned also; because the aforesaid residua, resulting from the experience of the pangs of death, is common to both the expert and the stupid.

Notes:—(1) "The learned," here are those that have studied the S'âstras theorietically, not those that have arrived at the truth; for as far as the latter are concerned, all trace of Ignorance is burnt up by the fire of wisdom, and as such there can be no distraction, which is only an effect of Ignorance.

The meaning of the Bhashya is thus put by Dr. Mitra: "It (*abhinivêśa*) proceeds from the memory of former experiences; and since none has in this life experienced the pain of death, it must follow that the fear of death is the result of the unconscious memory of the experience of a former state of life—and this fear is the cause of attachment to life."

Sutra (*10*) **These, the subtile ones, should be suppressed by retrogression.**

Com:—On the dissolution of the active mind of the Yogi, the aforesaid five distractions, having their seeds nearly burnt up, disappear together with it (the mind).

Notes:—(1) "*Dissolution*"—of the mind into its immediate cause, egoism. This dissolution of the effect into the cause, is what is meant by "retrogression;" and it may be added that this is only another name for Absolute meditation.

Of those that still continue, and have attained to the condition of the seed.—

Sutra (*11*):—Of these, the functions are to be suppressed by contemplation.

Com :—The gross functions of the distractions, having been attenuated by active yoga, are to be suppressed by contemplative wisdom, till they become Subtile, *i e.* till they have their seeds nearly burnt up. Just as the dust in a piece of cloth is at first shaken off, and the finer kinds then removed by finer means,—so in the same manner, the gross functions of the distractions have small adversaries, whereas the subtile ones have great adversaries.

Notes:—(1) "*That still continue*"—that are not yet burnt.

(2) "*Gross functions*"—those that are in active operation.

(3) "*Adversaries*"—*i.e.* means of suppression or destruction;—the small adversaries of the gross functions are to be—(1) attenuated by Active yoga, (2) have their seeds nearly burnt up by contemplative wisdom (and thus made subtile) and then lastly, (3) suppressed by retrogression—*i.e.* by Absolute meditation.

Sutra (*12*):—The residua of actions have their origin in distractions, and are felt in the manifest or the unmanifest life.

Com :—Of these, the residua of virtuous and vicious deeds give birth to desire, avarice, stupidity and anger; and this residuum is felt either by the manifest birth or by the unmanifest one. Of these that which is brought about by ardent repetition of mantras or by asceticism or by meditation,—or that which is accomplished by a proper attendance on (or devotion to) the great ones—The Lord, the elemental Gods, the great Rishis,—such a residuum of virtuous actions, bears immediate fruit. In the same manner, the repeated harms that are done to the fearing, the sick and the helpless, or to one who has confidence in the agent, or to the great ascetics —such a residuum of vicious actions also bears immediate fruit. As the Nandiśvara Kumara, having relinquished the human modification, was transformed into a god, and so also Nahusha the Lord of the gods, having relinquished his own form, was transformed into a beast. Of hellish beings there is no Karmic residuum which is felt in the manifest birth; and for those whose distractions have ended, there is no Karmic residuum to be felt in the unmanifest birth.

Notes.—*Manifest life* is the *present* life, and *unmanifest life* is the *future* life.

Sutra (13):—The root existing, its fruition (consists in) birth, life (or age) and experience.

Com:—It is only when the distractions exist that the Karmic residuum begins its fruition and not when the root in the shape of distractions has been destroyed. As for example, the rice in the paddy, is capable of sprouting up only when it is surrounded by the chaff, and has its seeding faculty undestroyed; and not when the chaff has been removed and the seeding faculty destroyed. Similarly the Karmic residuum is fit to sprout up into fruition only when hemmed in by distractions, and not when the distractions have been removed, or when its seeding faculty has been destroyed by the fire of wisdom.

This fruition is threefold. Birth, Age and Experience. In this connection we have to consider the following questions. Is a single action the cause of a single birth, or does a single action affect many births? and then arises the question.—Do many actions bring about many births; or do many actions bring about a single birth? Well, a single action cannot be said to be the cause of one birth. Why? Because in that case there would be no certainty of the succession of the results of present actions as well as of those innumerable remaining actions which have been heaping up through times immemorial; and as such people would lose all confidence (in the law of Karma *viz.*, actions always lead to retributive results) —which is far from desirable. Nor can a single action be the cause of many births; Why? Because in that case, from among (innumerable) past actions, a single action leading to many births, there would be no time for the fruition of the remaining actions;—and this too is not desirable. Nor can many actions be the cause of many births; Why? Because, it being impossible for the many births to occur simultaneously, we should postulate an order of succession for these; and this would lead to the former fault (*i.e.* the uncertainty in the order of succession, noted in connection with the first alternative).

For these reasons (we must hold that) the variegated residuum of all virtuous and vicious actions performed in the interval between birth and death, standing (among themselves) in the relation of the principal and the subsidiary, being manifested by death, and simultaneously joining together, accomplish death, and having thus become conjoined in one, bring about the one (following birth); and through the same unified action does this birth become equipped with its proper span of life; and the same action accomplishes the experience during this particular life. Thus then such a Karmic residuum, being the cause of birth, life and experience, is said to be "of three-fold function" It is for this reason that the Karmic residuum is said to be "*of one-birth*" *i.e.*, (whose effect is a single birth).

On the other hand, that which is felt by the manifest birth, being the cause of experience alone, is said to originate a single fruition; or when it is the cause of life and experience both, then it is said to originate a two-fold fruition as in the case of Nandîśvara or Nahusha. The residual longings (Vâsanâ) caused by the experience of the fruition of actions and distractions from time immemorial turn the mind into one aggregate whole; and the mind being thus variegated appears like a fishing net spread over with knots (which in the case of the mind would be the various residua as above described); thus are these residua said to be preceded by (caused by) many births. It is the Karmic residuum alone that is said to be of one birth. The impressions or tendencies (*sanskâras*), which cause the memory (or remembrance), are the residual longings (*Vâsanâ*), and are eternal.

The "one-birth" Karmic residuum is both of certain and uncertain fruition. Of these, this rule (the rule of being "of one birth") holds only in the case of the residuum experienced in the manifest birth, whose fruition is certain, and not in that of the residuum experienced in the manifest birth whose fruition is uncertain. Because in the case of the latter there are three courses: (1) The destruction of that which has been done, but has not borne results, (2) the inclusion (of the secondary ones) in the primary action, (3) the long continuity (of the secondary ones) as hemmed in by the primary action whose function is certain. As an example of the *first* we have the destruction in the present life of the black (evil) actions by the white (good) ones. In this connection it is declared "In this world actions are to be considered two-fold; the aggregate of good actions destroys the evil ones; therefore desire to perform good actions; the wise ones declare actions for thee in this present (birth)." To exemplify the *second*: "There may be little

(of evil), mixed up (with the good), removeable, and bearable; it is not capable of reducing the good ones ;—why? Because the quantity of the good is much, wherein this (evil) is hidden, and which is sure to bring about a slight harm even in heaven". (*Punchaśikhâcharya*). To exemplify the *third* course—"The long continuance of the secondary action hemmed in by the primary one whose fruition is certain"—How? Because it is only for the action experienced in the unmanifest birth, whose fruition is certain, that the cause of manifestation has already been said to be *death*, which is not the case with that which is experienced in unmanifest birth, and whose fruition is uncertain. This latter kind of actions may either be destroyed or dissolved (mixed up with the more important actions), or lastly long continue to exist as hemmed in (by those important actions),—so long as it is not turned towards fruition by its manifesting cause, in the form of some similar action. And it is for this uncertainty of the time, place and cause of the fruition of actions, that the course of action is said to be curious and unintelligible. As the secondary cannot be set aside by the primary, therefore we postulate the "One-birth" karmic residua.

Notes: (1) "*Lose all confidence*" *&c.*—The order of the fruition of Karmic residua being uncertain, the agent could not assure himself whether the evil or the good actions of his would produce results; and hence people would hesitate to give up a presently gratifying evil action for the sake of future happiness.

(2) "*The residual longings &c.*"—This anticipates the following objection. 'If the residual impressions too were "of one birth" like the Karmic residua, then the eternality of these longings (mentioned in aph. 10 Sec. 4) would become contradicted'. The sense of the reply is that the mind becoming variegated by the innumerable actions of various kinds, extending from time immemorial, these variegating residual longings must be regarded as belonging to "many births" and not confined, like Karmic residua, to "one birth" alone For if this were not the case, then a celestial or a bestial form after the human one, would not be explicable, as during human life it is

not possible to have such residual longings as would effect the divine or the bestial existence.

(3) "To exemplify the third .....How ?"—This question is based on the following doubt—'Death has been just said to be the only manifesting cause of Karmic residua, and now we find it asserted that the secondary action hemmed in by the primary one can long continue without fruition; and certainly as during this long-continuity, many deaths would intervene, the two assertions appear to contradict each other'. The sense of the reply is that the manifestation of the particular set of actions meant here, is due not to death, but to a different action similar in nature to the action in question.

Sutra (14):—They have pleasure or pain for their fruit, according as their cause is virtue or vice.

Com: "They "=birth, age and experience, having virtue for their cause, have pleasure for their fruit; and when they have vice for their cause, then they have pain for their fruit. As this pain consists in contrariness (to the agent's wishes), so also in the course of the pleasurable enjoyment of an object, there is pain for the yogi.

Note : (1) "*There is pain for the yogi*"—because pain has been defined as something that goes against the agent's wishes and as sensual pleasure is opposed to the yogi's wishes; so all sensual pleasure is really pain for him.

How do you explain this fact ? (Reply :)

Sutra (15) :—To the wise, all is pain,—because of the adverse functions of the Attributes, and of the pains of consequence, anxiety and impression.

Com: (I) The experience of pleasure, belonging to all persons, is infused with passion, and dependent upon animated and inanimate means; thus in this case there is the Karmic residua born of passion; similarly the agent avoids the means to pain, and is deluded (or infatuated),—so there is the Karmic residuum born of aversion and stupefaction. As is declared: "No enjoyment is possible without killing some beings",—thus there is the bodily Karmic residuum born of the slaughter, and it has already been declared that all sensual pleasure is Ignorance, pleasure consists in the peace resulting from the satisfaction of the senses with regard to sensuous objects, and pain consists in the want of peace resulting from fickleness. And certainly the satisfaction of the senses cannot be brought about by repeated enjoyment; why? Because the passions grow by repeated enjoyment, as does also the pertness of the senses. Consequently repeated enjoyment cannot be the means of pleasure. Thus then if a person desiring pleasure, is infused with (a desire for) sensuous objects and hence becomes entangled in the mire of pain,—it affords a parallel to the case of one who, fearing the bite of the common scorpion, is stung by a serpent. This "pain of consequence" (i. e. the pain that follows as a result of pleasure), being contrary (to the wish), troubles the yogi even in a state of pleasure, (because he knows that it will end in pain).

II Now, what is the nature of the "pain of anxiety"? All men have the experience of anxiety, infused with aversion, and depending upon animate and inanimate causes—thus there is Karmic residuum born of aversion; and again with a view to the means of pleasure, the agent acts by body, words and mind, and thereby favours or harms another; and this favouring or harming of others brings about an aggregate of virtue and vice,—this Karmic residuum proceeds from avarice and delusion; and this is what is called the "pain of anxiety."

What is the "pain of impressions"? The residuum of pleasurable impressions proceeds from an experience of pleasure and that of painful impressions from the experience of pain.

Similarly, when either pleasure or pain is experienced, as fruits of actions, then again follows the stock of Karmic residuum. Thus this everlasting flow of the current of pain, consisting in contrariness (to his wishes), makes the yogi anxious; why ? Because the wise is like the eye-ball; just as a fine thread of wool put in the eye gives pain by mere touch, which it does not do in other parts of the body, so do the aforesaid pains give pain to the eye-ball-like yogi alone, and to no other agent. On the other hand, the agent who relinquishes the pain caused by his own actions which he has borne,and again bears that which has been relinquished,—and who is on all sides hemmed in by Ignorance as it were in the form of the mental function variegated by everlasting residual longings,–and lastly, who has the idea of 'self' and 'mine' with regard to the objects to be avoided (the body, wife and children &c),—such an agent, whenever he is born, is flooded over by threefold pain, brought about both by extrinsic and intrinsic causes. Thus then, seeing his own self as well as all other beings hemmed in by the everlasting current of pain, the yogi takes refuge in proper Descrimination, which has the power of destroying all pain.

For the further reason of "the adverse character of the functions of the Attributes, all is pain to the wise." The Attributes of the Buddhi consisting in enlightenment, action (or energy) and idleness, depending upon mutual help, give rise to the quiescent, passionate or delusive cognition, partaking of (the character of) the three Attributes. And the functioning of the Attributes being fickle, the mind is said to be quickly modifying. The *forms* as well as the *functions*, in their excess, are contradictory to one another; whereas those that are in their ordinary condition cooperate with those that are in excess. Thus, these Attributes, depending upon one another, bring about the ideas of pleasure, pain and delusion; therefore each of them has the character of all the three; their difference depending upon the predominance and subserviency (of one or the other of them). And thus all is pain to the wise.

Of this aggregate of pains, the productive seed is Ignorance; and the cause of the absence of this is Right Discrimination. As the science of medicine has four parts—viz : the disease, the cause of the disease, cure, and medicine,—so this science also has four parts–viz : metempsychosis (birth), the cause of this, Liberation, and the means of liberation; and of these, Metempsychosis, abounding in pain, is to be avoided; the connection of Matter and Spirit is the cause of what is to be avoided; the removal of the connection consists in absolute and final separation; and the cause of this separation is Right Discrimination. In this connection, the form of the avoiding agent can not be said to be either avoided or accepted; for if it were avoided, that would lead to the theory of self-annihilation; and if it were accepted, then it would lead to the "cause" theory; (consequently) by denying both (avoidability and acceptability) we land on the theory of the "eternal", which constitutes right discrimination.

Notes (1) "*Animate and inanimate*"—wife and children, and beds and clothes &c.

(2) "*Infatuated*"—on account of not being able to discard them.

(3) "*No enjoyment without killing &c*"—Cf. the "पञ्चसूना गृहस्थस्य" such as the death of insects &c. caused in cooking and so on.

(4) "*It has been declared.........Ignorance*"—supply "by us, at the time of explaining the four forms of Ignorance."

(5) "*Pleasure consists &c*"—wise people do not wish for that which gives only temporary pleasure; what they strive after is permanent pleasure in the end, and not after the temporary pleasure which ends in pain—Cf. the Bhagavadgitâ–विषयेन्द्रियसंयोगात् &c. Pleasure consists in contentment, and it is continued dissatisfaction alone which renders even pleasures painful. Cf. Bhartrihari—

स भवति धनहीनो यस्य तृष्णा विशाला मनसि च परितुष्टे कोऽर्थवान् को दरिद्रः" ।

"*The pain of anxiety*"—Vachaspati *Miśra* remarks that the commentator does not go into the details of this because it is too well known to need any dilatory expounding; and more so because the pain of anxiety is similar to that of "Consequence" mentioned before,—the reason for mentioning them separately is that the pain of anxiety differs from that of consequence in as much as the former is painful all along, in the beginning, in the middle and in the end, whereas the latter is painful only at the end.

(6) "*Passions grow by repeated enjoyment*"—Cf. Manu—

न जातु कामः कामानामुपभोगेन शाम्यति
हविषा कृष्णवर्त्मेव भूयस्वाभिवर्धते ॥

(8) "*The forms and functions in their excess &c*"—The "forms" are the eight forms of Buddhi—viz: (1) virtue, wisdom, dispassion, power, vice, ignorance, passion and imbecility; and the functions are three—viz: pleasure, pain and delusion. The sense is that it is only when all of these are in the height of their power and equally ready for function, that they contradict one another—E. G. when both virtue and vice are in power, then they contradict each other; if however one of them is in its ordinary form, then it co-operates with the stronger one. This has been added in anticipation of the objection that a single entity cannot be pleasurable and painful as well as delusive. The meaning is—"There is hardly any one thing which is not made of these three qualities, as obviously there is nothing which is free from being the source of pleasure, pain and delusion to different parties, and (at times) by turns to the same party." (M. N. Dvivedi). All objects are made up of the three Attributes; the only difference being that the object that is pleasurable at first sight is abounding in the quality of goodness and so on. [In this connection, the reader must look up the *Sânkhya—Tattva—Kaumudi*, under Kârikâs: XII and XIII].

(9) "*The form of the avoiding agent &c.*": If the form of the agent—i.e. the self—were avoided or suppressed, there would result the annihilation of self, and certainly no sane person would strive after such self-annihilation. Secondly, if it were accepted (effected); then it would follow that being a caused entity, it must have a cause, and be an effect, and thus transient and destructible; and this theory would do away with Liberation which means only Immortality; and certainly no immortality would be possible for the *caused* self. Thirdly if both the above alternatives were denied, then would self come to be eternal.

["The object of this aphorisim is to establish that everything connected with worldly life is painful, and the yogis should therefore shun them all. To prove this it is first shown that all joyous actions are followed by pain. There must be a change after the enjoyment of pleasure; and as there is an increase of desire from enjoyment, there must be frequent disappointments, and they inflict pain even in the act of enjoyment; there is always a dread of something that may disturb it, and so it is not unalloyed. Then all actions and all impressions leave behind residua in the field of the thinking principle, and they revive sensations of pleasure and pain. And lastly, the three qualities are adverse to each other, and therefore they create disturbances and cause pain. The conclusion is a state of pessimism, from which the only relief is to be had by totally cutting himself off from all worldly affairs. This pessimism forms the basis of all the leading systems of Indian Philosophy, and is not unknown to Europe."

(*Mitra.*)

The four-foldness of this Science is now explained:

Sutra (16): Avoidable is the pain not yet come.

Com:—The pain that has passed has already been spent up by Experience, and as such cannot come within the range of avoidability. The pain that is present is, during the moment of its existence, ready for experience, and as such cannot at any other moment, be avoided For this reason it is that pain alone which is not yet come, that gives pain to the eye-ball-like yogi, and none else; and it is this pain that is to be warded off.

The cause of that which is to be avoided is now laid down:

Sutra (17):—The conjunction of the Spectator and the Spectacle is the cause of that which is to be warded off.

Com:—"The Spectator"=the Spirit, the cogniser of ***Buddhi***; "The Spectacle"=All the properties that exist in the "goodness" of Buddhi. Such a spectacle, resembling a magnet, and operating by mere proximity, through its visibility comes to be the Spirit's "*own*"—(the spirit being) the Lord, of the form of (pure) consciousness. (Because) The ***Sâttvic Buddhi*** (consciousness) becomes the object of experience and action (of the Spirit); and acquiring its existence through another form, becomes dependent upon another, though by itself it is independent, on account of its being for another's purpose. Of these two, the spectator and the spectacle, the connection brought about for a purpose, is the cause of that which is to be avoided *i.e.*—of pain. And it has been declared: "By avoiding the cause in the shape of connection therewith (with Buddhi) this would be an absolute remedy for pain"-(Panchaśikha). Why? Because, we know the remedy for the cause of pain, the avoidable—e. g. the sores of the feet being capable of being pierced, and the thorn being capable of piercing, the remedy hereof lies in not putting the foot on a thorn, or putting it on it, doing so with shoes. One who knows these three facts, and has recourse to the remedy, does not experience the pain caused by the pricking of the thorn. Why? Because of the capability of recognizing the threefoldness. Similarly with regard to the case in question, the Attribute of goodness is the *object of pain* caused by that of foulness, the *causer of pain*—Why? Because the action of *paining* must fall on an *object*; and the action of paining (in the present instance) falls on the object of the attribute of Goodness; and not on the Cogniser (the Spirit) who is non-modificable and devoid of action. Because the Spirit has objects presented to himself (by Buddhi), therefore when the attribute of goodness (the spiritual consciousness) is afflicted, the Spirit too, on account of His dependence on its form, becomes afflicted.

Notes:—(1) "*Such a spectacle ressembling a magnet &c.*":—It has already been explained under aph. 4, Sec. I, how the Sattvic Buddhi, though untouched by the sentient faculty, yet through its clearness, taking in the reflection thereof, appears as if endowed with intelligence, and as such experiences the various objects of sense. And it is for this reason that the spectator enjoys the pleasure *etc.* presented to himself by the consciousness which has taken the form of the particular objects of sense. And such a spiritual consciousness becomes his own form, as it were. Because it becomes the object of the spectator's experience and action, on account of its existing at that time, *its another form*" ; and so though naturally independent, it becomes dependent on the spirit, on account of its being for another's purpose. The author has added "in another form," in anticipation of the objection that spiritual consciousness being naturally-illuminative, cannot be the object of any experience &c. The sense of the reply (implied by the epithet *Anyasvarûpêṇa* &c.) is that if the consciousness were really of the form of inteligence, then only would it be self-illuminative ; but as a matter of fact it "has its existence in a *form which is other than that of intelligence*"—*i.e.* the non-intelligent form-its apparent intelligence being due to the reflection therein of the spirit's intelligence. And as such it is quite fit to become the object of the spirit's experience.

(2) "*The attribute of goodness is the object of pain*" *&c.*—This is in anticipation of the following objection :—"In the example cited we have three members—(1) the pierced foot (2) the piercing thorn, and (3) the remedy, the wearing of shoes. But in the case in question, we do not find three members, because it is the Buddhi alone which is both the afflictor and the afflicted (as the pain is caused by the foulness of the Buddhi and is experienced also by the Buddhi, whose afflictions the spirit takes upon himself); and so there is no parallellism, between the instance and the point at issue". The sense of the reply is that here also we have three members—(1) the afflictor, in the shape of foulness, (2) the afflicted in that of Goodness, and (3) the remedy, the separation of Buddhi from the Spirit—That is to say, though Buddhi is one, yet it is threefold, being made up of the three Attributes. The reasons for not making the spirit, the *afflicted*, are next given ; the chief of which is that, being unmodifiable, the spirit can never be the substrate of any action ; and as such the action of 'pain' falls not upon Him, but on the modifying Buddhi ; but in as much as the spirit depends for his experience, on the form of Buddhi wherein his itelligence is reflected,—*He* appears as if He himself were the *afflicted*.

The form of the Spectacle is now described :

Sutra (18):—The spectacle is of the nature of illumination, activity and inertia; it consists of the elements and the sense-organs ; it is for the purpose of experience and emancipation.

Com:—"Goodness" is of the nature of "illumination"; "Foulness" of the nature of "activity," and "Darkness" of the nature of "inertia." Thus, these Attributes principally coloured by one another, having the properties of (and capable of) connection and separation, with their respective forms accomplished by mutual help,—and though mutually subservient yet, having their respective capabilities unmixed,—capable of wielding their capabilities with regard to homogeneous and hetergeneous effects—having their respective proximity(functions)manifested at the time of their respective predominance (activity or operation)—and though *gunas* (subservient) yet, having their existence inferred as included in the primary,—having these faculties employed in the accomplishment of the spirit's ends —helping by mere proximity, and thus resembling a piece of magnet,—and even in the absence of any predisposing causes (such as virtue and the rest), following in the wake of any one of themselves (the one that happens to be the predominating attribute with regard to the effect in question),—come to be denoted by the name of *Pradhâna* (Primordial Matter), ; and this is also called the "spectacle."

This "Spectacle" "consists of the elements and the sense—organs" ;—*i.e.* modifying in the form of the elements, *i.e.*, the earth and the rest, in their gross as well as subtile forms ; and similarly modifying into the form of the sense-organs—the ear and the rest, in their gross as well as subtile forms. This is not without a purpose; on the contrary it operates only with a view to a distinct purpose ; consequently, the spectacle is "for the purpose of the experience and emancipation" of the Spirit. Of these, "experience" consists in the ascertainment of the forms of the desirable and the undesirable, not differentiated ; and "emancipation" is the ascertainment of the nature of the experience. Besides these two, there is no other perception. As is declared,—"Even on the existence of three active Attributes, he (the unwise one) recognises the various natural dispositions (virtue &c.) as presented to the fourth, the inactive—Spirit, similar as well as dissimilar (to the attributes), the witness of their operations ; and as such does not think any other form of perception possible."—(*Panchasikha*).

(Question :) How are these two, experience and emancipation,— brought about as they are by Buddhi, and also existing therein—referred to the Spirit ? (Reply :) Just as victory or defeat, really belonging to the fighting soldiers, are referred to their master ; because he enjoys the fruits thereof ; so also bondage and emancipation, really belonging to the Buddhi, are referred to the Spirit, because He is the enjoyer of the fruits of both. Bondage is the non-accomplishment of the soul's purpose, belonging to the Buddhi ; and the accomplishment of the same purpose constitutes emancipation. By this (it is established that) perception, memory, inference or assumptions (*Uha*), (*Apòha*), right knowledge, attachment —all belonging to Buddhi, are assumed to exist in the Spirit ; because he is the enjoyer of the fruits of these.

Notes :—"*Though mutually subservient &c*"—Though on the occasion of an effect abounding in peace (hence an effect of the goodness principally) foulness and darkness have subordinate places, yet this does not give rise to an admixture of their functions. Though everything is a product of the three attributes, yet in a peaceful object, the predominating influence is that of goodness; and so on.

(2) "*Homogeneous and &c.*"—Though the principal material cause is necessarily homogeneous, yet, the auxilliary and the secondary causes are heterogeneous also.

(3) "*At the time of their respective predominance*"—If the effect to be produced be a divine body then the predominating attribute is that of goodness ; in case of a human body, that of foulness, and in the case of a bestial body, that of darkness ; in each case the secondary causes being the other two attributes. "Pradhâna"="Pradhânatva."

(4) "*And though subservient &c.*"—This is said in anticipation of the following objection:—"The predominating attribute, having come forward, may be the capable one, but how does that prove the existence of its auxilliaries?" The sense of the reply is that though the auxilliaries have not yet come forward, yet their existence as included in the

Primary one is inferred on account of the nature of the attributes being such that they are never disconnected from each after, and always act conjointly with one another.

(5) "*Even on the existence &c,,*"—A quotation from Panchasikha. The Spirit is dissimilar to the Attributes in as much as He is free from the attributes, and is discriminative, non-objective, and non-productive &c., and He is Similar to them in as much as he is, with them, uncaused, eternal &c., (cf. *Sânkhya-Kârikâ*—त्रिगुणमविवेकि ......ताद्विपरीतस्तथा च पुमान् ॥

(6) "*He is the enjoyer.*"—Spirit, as the enjoyer, has been explained in aph. 4, sec I, and will be described in aph. 34, Sec. III. (For parallel passages from the Smritis see, Yogavârtika and Tippaṇi p. 146.)

Now begins the consideration of the ascertainment of the different forms of the Attributes, which make up the "Spectacle."—

Sutra (19):—The specific and the unspecific, the solely mergent, and the non-mergent—are the stages of the Attributes.

Com:—Of these, Âkâsa, Air, Fire, Water and Earth, the five elements are the *specific* (directly evolved effects) of the *unspecific* sound, touch colour taste and odour (respectively). Similarly the ear, the skin, the eye, the tongue and the nostril,—the sensational sense-organs,—as also speech, the hands, the feet, and the two excretory organs—the five organs of action,—and lastly the universal *mind*—(all these eleven) are the specific (effects) of the unspecific form of Self-consciousness. This sixteen-fold specific modification belongs to the Attributes. The "unspecific" are six: viz: the rudimentary sound, the rudimentary touch, the rudimentary colour, the rudimentary taste, and the rudimentary odour,—having respectively one, two, three, four and five characterestics are the five "unspecific;" and the sixth is

Self-consciousness, pure and simple. These are the unspecific modifications of Mahat (=Buddhi or consciousness) itself, which is capacity (capability of fulfilling the soul's purpose) pure and simple—That which is above the unspecific —is the "solely mergent" spiritual consciousness,—in this, taking their stand, the unspecific modifications reach their highly developed states; and also when dissolving, they take their stand, in the same simple capacity, on the spiritual consciousness, and finally resolve themselves into the unmanifested and non-mergent primordrial Matter, (Nature) which is beyond existence and non-existence, as also beyond the existing and the non-existing (effects.)

This (consciousness) is the "solely mergent" modification of the Attributes; and the "non-mergent" modification is that which is beyond capacity and incapacity. In the non-mergent condition, the soul's purpose is not the cause; because in the beginning of the non-mergent condition the soul's purpose does not act as the propelling cause; therefore the soul's purpose is not the cause thereof. And because this is not brought about by the soul's purpose, therefore it is called "eternal." In the begining of the three particular states (the solely mergent, the unspecific and the specific) the propelling is by the soul's purpose, which becomes their cause; whence these three are called "non-eternal." The Attributes on the other hand, partaking of the properties of all of these, neither dissolve, nor are produced. They however appear as if endued with the properties of birth and dissolution, through (their connection with) the different individuals, past, present & future, which have the property of connecting themselves with the Attributes; just as Devadatta is said to be becoming poor or deteriorating, because his cattle are dying; so it is only the death of the cattle, and not the destruction of his own form, that constitutes his poverty. This case is exactly similar (to that of the apparent birth and death of the Attributes.)

The solely mergent, existing in close proximity to the non-mergent, and originating therein, becomes divided therefrom,—because of the infringibility of the order of sequence; for certainly the sequence is never broken; similarly the six unspecific modifications originating in the solely mergent become divided therefrom in accordance with the fixed order of sequence of the modifications. In the same manner, the elements and the sense—organs, originating in these unspecific ones, become divided therefrom. As has been declared above: "There is nothing beyond the specific"—*i. e.*, of the specific there is no further modification into any other object. Later on, we shall explain their modification into a condition characterised by virtue.

Notes:—(1) *Having, one, two, &c.*" The sound has the characteristic of sound alone, touch that of touch and sound, colour that of colour touch and sound, taste that of taste and the preceding three, and lastly odour of odour and the preceding four.

(2) "*Mahat itself &c.*": 'Itself' is added in order to show the relative importance of *Mahat*.

(3) "*Beyond existence &c*": The meaning is that the three attributes in equilibrium (which is Prakriti) are not capable of fulfilling the soul's ends, and as such Prakriti is said to be "beyond existence" —*i. e.*, without the capacity spoken of above; nor is it merely a hypothetical assumption, not really existing, hence it is said to be "beyond non-existence."

(4) "*Devadatta &c.*"—Just as the improvement or otherwise of the cattle is an attribute to the owner (who is not directly connected with the improvement or otherwise); so the origin and dissolution of the various modifications appear as if belonging to their cause, the Attributes.

(5) "The infringibility of the order of sequence"—The order is thus laid down in the Sânkhya-Kârikâ: प्रकृतेर्महांस्ततोऽहंकारस्तस्माद्गणश्च षोडशकः (From Prakriti, Mahat, from Mahat, self-consciousness; and from this

last the sixteen"); and since this order can never be broken, the "solely-mergent," Buddhi (mahat) is the immediate modification of the Primordial matter.

The "spectacle" has been described; now commences the determination of the form of the "spectator."

Sutra (20):—The spectator is absolute sentience, and though pure, (still) beholds intellected ideas.

Com:—"Absolute sentience"=*i. e.* the faculty of perception pure and simple, unalloyed with qualifications (illumination); this is the counter-cogniser of consciousness. He is neither similar nor dissimilar to it. He is not similar. Why? Because consciousness appertaining to known as well as unknown objects, is modifiable; its objects—cow, jar and the like,—being known and unknown, prove it to be modifying. The fact of the Spirit having every object always known to him implies his unmodifying character. Why? Because, (1) consciousness, which is also the object of the Spirit, cannot be both the perceiver and the non-perceiver. Thus is established the fact of every object being always known to the Spirit; which further proves his unmodifying nature. And further (secondly) consciousness is for another's purpose, because of its operating conjointly (with the sense-organs, the sensuous objects and self-consciousness); the Spirit on the other hand, exists for his own purpose. And (*thirdly*) again consciousness, being capable of ascertaining all the objects, (peaceful, passionate or dark), is made up of the three Attributes, and as such, is insentient; the Spirit on the other hand is the spectator of the three Attributes. For these reasons the Spirit is not similar to conciousness. Then let it be dissimilar. No; it is not altogether dissimilar either. Why? Because "though pure, still it beholds intellected ideas"—*i. e.*, because it perceives the ideas belonging to consciousness; and thus *perceiving* appears similar to it, though really it is not so; as has been declared. "The faculty of the experiencing agent, unmodifying and non-transferable, appears as if transferred to the modifying object, and falls in with the function there of; and (the same faculty),—endued only with an imitation of the Buddhic function which has been coloured by the touch of sentience,—and as such really untainted by the Buddhic functions,—is called the function of *knowledge*"—*Panchasikhâchârya.*

Notes:—"*Though pure, still beholds &c.*," cf I—4.

Sutra (21):—Only for his purpose is the being of the spectacle.

Com:—The spectacle becoming the object of the Spirit whose form is sentience pure and simple,—the being *i.e.*, the form of the spectacle is for his purpose. On the accomplishment of experience and emancipation, the (insentient) form of the spectacle, attaining to its existence through another form (the sentient form of the spirit reflected therein), is no longer seen by the Spirit. The destruction of the form would lead to the destruction of the spectacle; but it is not *destroyed.*

Notes: (1) *The "destruction &c."* The objection means that the spectacle being one and the same for all spirits (on account of Nature being one), if it is destroyed in the case of one, it must be so in the case of all, and this would create the anomaly of the emancipation of a single spirit bringing about that of all others. The reply is that the spectacle is *not destroyed* for the emancipated Spirit; he only ceases to perceive it; and his sentience not being reflected in Buddhi, he ceases to feel any pleasure or pain &c., the results of his connection with the Attributes of Buddhi. Cf. *Sânkhya—Karika.* दृष्टा मयेत्युपेक्षकएको दृष्टाऽहमित्युपरमत्यन्या इति ॥

Why?

Sutra (22):—**Destroyed in the case of one whose purpose has been fulfilled, it is not destroyed, for she is common to others besides him.**

Com:—Though the spectacle is destroyed with regard to the one Spirit whose purpose has been fulfilled, yet it is not destroyed, because it is common to other spirits. Though it is destroyed with regard to the expert soul, still not having its purpose fulfilled with regard to the inexpert ones, it becomes the object of the sentience of these latter; and as such it still continues to acquire its existence through another's. Thus the faculties of the seer and the seen being eternal, their ever-lasting connection has been described. As has been declared:—"The objects possessing certain properties being eternal, the connection of the properties themselves too is eternal."

The next aphorism has been called forth by a desire to lay down the form of the conjunction (just spoken of):—

Sutra (23):—**Conjunction is the cause of the recognition of the natures of the faculties of itself and that of its Lord's.**

Com:—The Spirit, the Lord, becomes conjoined with his spectacle, for the sake of perception. Hence, the apprehension of the spectacles through such a conjunction is *experience*; on the other hand the recognition of the nature of the spectator is *emancipation*. The conjunction having its end in perception, this latter is said to be the cause of disjunction; and non-perception being contradictory to perception, it is said to be the cause of conjunction. Here perception is not the cause of emancipation, because the absence of non-perception leads to the absence of bondage; and this is *emancipation.* And because the existence of perception leads to its negation, non-perception, the cause of bondage,—therefore the cognition of perception is said to be the cause of Isolation.

Now, what is this 'non-perception'? (1) Is it a previleged office of the Attributes? or (2) is it the non-production of the principal mind which has presented objects to its sentient Lord *i. e.* the want of perception in his spectacle? or (3) is it the fact of the attributes resting in the purpose (experience and emancipation)? or (4) Ignorance with its mind being suppressed (*i. e.*, becoming similar to its cause, Nature), is the productive seed (in the form Vásaná) of its mind (and thus in this case non-perception being the residual longing of Ignorance)? or (5) on the destruction of the impression (Sanskâra) of fixity (*sthiti*), the manifestation of the impression of motion? In this connection it has been declared: "The Pradhâna, continuing in its fixity, and as such not producing any modifications, would become the non-Pradhâna (*i. e.*, the non-cause, the inefficient cause); similarly continuing in its mobility, its modifications would become eternal, and thus too would it become non-Pradhâna (because the character of the Pradhâna consists in producing modifications and thence affording experience for the spirit, and in time dissolving it, and bringing about his emancipation). It is only when it operates both ways (both by fixity and mobility), that it is called Pradhána, not otherwise. The same consideration holds respecting other causes. Or (6) the power of the spectacle (experience &c.,) alone is non-perception—so say some; on the strength of the Sruti: "The operation of the Pradhána is for the information of the soul." The spirit capable of apprehending all that is to be cognised, does not perceive anything, prior to the operation of Nature; and then too the spectacle, which is capable of producing all effects, is not perceived; and this is non-perception. (7) Some people assert that non-perception is the property of both (the spectator spirit, and the spectacle). In this case the perception of the spectacle, though constituting its very nature, is yet recognised as the property of the spectacle only through the cognition of the spirit (because without the reflection of the sentience of the spirit, no conscious perception is possible); similarly though the perception does not constitute the nature of the spirit, yet it appears to be the property of the spirit, through the cognition of the spectacle (because without the reflecting spectacle no perception is possible). (8) Lastly, some people assert non-perception to be the consciousness of the perception.

All these alternatives are mere fancies of the scientific mind. In this connection, the great number of alternatives has a common object in reference to the conjunction of all the souls with the attributes.

The conjunction of the retrogade sentience with its own spiritual consciousness (is such that)

Sutra (24) :—its cause is Ignorance;

Com :—that is, the residual longings of misconceived ideas. Spiritual consciousness, coloured by the residual longings of misconceived notions, attains to the effectual condition of spiritual discrimination, and again returns (to its operations) with full-pledged powers. When however it ends in spiritual discrimination, then it attains its highest limit of effectiveness and having its office thus fulfilled it ceases to act; and hence being devoid of perception, does not return to its operation, there being no cause of bondage.

A certain person (the Nihilist) jokes at emancipation through the example of an impotent husband:—"The impotent person being exhorted by his young wife in this manner—My dear, my sister has children, wherefore have I not got any ?—replies to her thus : 'when I am dead, then will I produce children for thee.' In the same manner the knowledge when present not accomplishing the suppression of the mind, what hope is there of its accomplishing it when it itself will have been destroyed?" In reply to this says a certain sect of the masters (of our Science) : "The suppression of the consciousness itself constitutes emancipation, the said suppression resulting from the absence of the cause of non-perception,—this non-perception, the cause of bondage, disappearing on (right) perception."

Thus then it is the suppression of the mind that constitutes emancipation; and as such, wherefore this inopportune mental aberration (of the Nihilist.)

Note :—(1) This aphorism decides in favour of the *fourth* out of the eight alternatives just noticed.

That which is to be warded off is pain, the cause of which has been declared to be Conjunction together with its causes. Now it remains to describe the process of avoidance.

Sutra (25) :—**From its absence, there is absence of conjunction, (which is) avoidance ; and that is the Isolation of the spectator.**

Com :—From the absence of non-perception, there is absence of the conjunction of the spirit and spiritual consciousness,—that is to say, the absolute cessation of bondage. This is "avoidance," and "it is the isolation of the spectator"—that is, the non-mixture of the spirit, the non-conjunction with the attributes. On the disappearance of the cause of pain, there is cessation of pain which is (its) avoidance ; and after this, the spirit abides in his own form.

Now, what is the means for getting at this avoidance?

***Sutra* (26) :—Undisturbed discriminative knowledge is the means of avoidance.**

Com :—"Discriminative knowledge" is the recognition of the difference between the Spirit and the Attributes. And this knowledge becomes disturbed by the non-cessation of false knowledge. When however this false knowledge has its seeding faculty burnt up, and as such ceases to procreate, then flows the lucid current of the discriminative knowledge belonging to Goodness (sattva), free from the impurities of pain, and abiding in supreme wisdom, the high pedestal of *Vaśîkâra* Dispassion (*vide above*). And this undisturbed discriminative knowledge is the cause of avoidance, whence follows the burning up of the seeding faculty of false knowledge, which thus ceases to procreate. This is the highway of Emancipation, the means of the avoidance (of pain).

***Sutra* (27) :—For him the consciousness to the utmost stage is seven-fold.**

Com :—" For him " refers to one who has discriminative knowledge. " *Seven-fold* "—On the removal of the enveloping impurities of Buddhi, no further cognition being brought about,—the consciousness of the wise one becomes only seven-fold. These grades are :—(1) The avoidable has been known, there is nothing more of it to be known ; (2) the causes of the avoidable (pain) have been attenuated, there is nothing more of them to be attenuated; (3) the avoidance has been directly perceived by means of suppressive meditation; (4) the means of avoidance in the shape of discriminative knowledge has been accomplished. Such is the fourfold effected end of consciousness. The end of mind again is threefold: (1) The office of spiritual consciousness has been fulfilled; (2) the attributes devoid of rest like stones fallen from the mountain-top, turned towards dissolution into their cause, disappear together therewith; and of these dissolved ones there is no more production, for want of any purpose—(3) in this state, the spirit, outgrowing all attributive connection, pure and shining in his own pristine form, becomes isolated.

The spirit, witnessing this sevenfold consciousness, to its utmost stage, is called "Adept." And even on the retrogade procreation of the mind, he is emancipated and becomes "adept." because of his having gone beyond the range of the attributes.

Discriminative knowledge becomes the means to avoidance, only when fully accomplished; and since this accomplishment is not possible without some means, therefore now commences the consideration of such means.

Sutra (28):—On the decay of impurity through the practice of the accessories of yoga, there is an enlightenment of consciousness, till discriminative knowledge is accomplished.

Com:—"Accessories of yoga": the eight, about to be described; through the practice of these, results the decay of impurity in the shape of the fivefold misconception; and on this decay, results the manifestation of right knowledge. As the accessories come to be practised, the impurity becomes gradually attenuated; and as this decay, so is the increase of the brightness of consciousness, dependent upon the order of the decay ; and this brightness goes on gradually increasing "till discriminative knowledge results"—that is to say till the recognition of the nature of the Spirit and the Attributes.

The practice of the accessories of Yoga is the cause of the disjunction of impurity, as the axe is of the (disjunction of the) object cut ; and it is the cause of the attainment of discriminative knowledge, as virtue is of pleasure ; and in no other way can it be a cause. How many are these causes said to be in science ? They are nine—*e. g.* (1) Utpattikârana the originative (2) "Sthitikarana (fixitive), (3) "abhivyaktikarana" (manifestive), (4) "vikârakarana" (modificatory), (5) "Pratyayakarana" (cognitive), (6) "Âptikarana" (approaching), (7) "Viyogakarana" (disjunctive), (8) "Anyatvakarana" (Differentiative), and (9) "Dhritikarana (up-holding). To exemplify these severally—(1) the mind of consciousness; (2) the soul's purpose of the mind, and food of the body; (3) light and the consciousness thereof, of form or colour; (4) other objects, of the mind, and fire of the food to be cooked; (5) the knowledge of smoke, of the knowledge of fire; (6) the practice of yogic accessories, of discriminative knowledge; (7) the same practice, of impurity; (8) the goldsmith of the gold; and similarly of a single mental function [=*vritti* (feminine)], Ignorance is the cause of its stupefaction; aversion of its painfulness, desire of its pleasurableness, true knowledge of its impartiality; (9) the body of the sense-organs, and *vice versa*, the great elements of the bodies, and these latter of one another,—the animal, the human and the divine bodies upholding one another. These are the nine causes. As occasion presents itself, these are to be applied to other objects also. But the causal efficiency of the practice of the accessories of yoga is only twofold (*i. e.*, the *disjunctive* and the *procuring*, as mentioned above, before the enunciation of the forms of causality).

The accessories of yoga are next described :

Sutra (29) :—**Restraint (or Forbearance), Observance, Posture, Regulation of Breath, Abstraction, Concentration, Contemplation, and Meditation—are the eight accessories.**

Com :—We shall now describe in due order, the form and practice of these.

Sutra (30):—**Forbearance consists in harmlessness truth, abstinence from theft, continence and freedom from avarice.**

Com :—Of these "harmlessness"=in no way and at no time wishing ill to any living being. The following restraints and observances have all of them abstinence for their root, and being included in its accomplishment, are performed only for the proper performance thereof ;—*i. e.*, they are practised only in order to clarify the aforesaid abstinence. It has been thus declared : "As the Brâhmaṇa performs many penances, so does he become alienated from the cause of harm to others and thus brings about the same harmlessness duly clarified."

"Truth"—consists in word and mind corresponding to facts—that is word and mind both tallying with objects as seen, inferred or heard (from authentic sources). A word is spoken for the transference of one's thought to another, and as such if it is not deceptive or mistaken, or devoid of comprehension (unable to be comprehended by the listener), (then it is *true*);—it is so only when it is used for the good of others, and not for their evil. If being spoken as such (as a truth) it leads to the injury of others, then it would not be truth; it would be a sin; and by this semblance of virtue (the agent) would suffer endless trouble. Therefore one ought to tell the truth with a due consideration of the good of all beings.

Theft consists in the acceptance of objects from others, in a manner contrary to the prescribed forms (of gift). The abstinence from this in the shape of absence of desire therefor, is "*Astéya.*"

"Continence"—the control of the secret generative organs.

"Freedom from avarice" consists in the non-acceptance of any objects, on account of a due sense of the discrepancies therein, in the shape of trouble attendant upon its acquirement, protection, waste or consumption, attachment, and malevolence (towards other competitors).

Notes :—"*Truth*"—Cf. Manu:

सत्यं ब्रूयात् प्रियं ब्रूयान्न ब्रूयात् सत्यमप्रियम् ॥
प्रियञ्च नानृतं ब्रूयात् एष धर्मः सनातनः ॥

These, however, are—

Sutra (31) :—the Great Penance, when in all stages, the above are not conditioned by (*are irrespective of*) class, place, time and convention.

Com :—of these, harmlessness conditioned (or limited) by class—the killing of fish, and nothing else, by fishermen (which is wrongly tolerated by people). "Conditioned by place"—as 'I will not kill in a sacred place'; "conditioned by time"—'I will not kill on the 14th day of the fortnight or on other sacred days; and lastly the harmlessness "conditioned by convention," [belonging to one who is above the three kinds of "slaughter" just mentioned],—as "I shall kill (animals) for the sake of the gods and the Brahmanas, and not otherwise;" or again killing is allowable for the warrior caste, in battle, and nowhere else. Harmlessness and the rest, not conditioned by these—class, place, time and convention—are to be always practised, in all stages—*i. e.*, with regard to all objects; and thus being free from any sort of restriction, they are called the Great Penance, belonging to all stages.

***Sutra* (32) :—The observances are—purification, contentment, penance, study and devotion to the Lord.**

Com :—Of these, "purification" the *external*, consists in the removal of impure objects by means of clay and water &c., and the *internal*, in the removal of the impurities of the mind. "Contentment"—the absence of any desire for acquiring things other than those that are near at hand. "Penance"—the bearing of the "pair of opposites,"—such as hunger and thirst, heat and cold, sitting and standing, complete and formal silence (the former consisting in not expressing one's ideas even by gestures, and the latter in mere absence of articulate speech); and the penances proper, are the *Krichhra* the *Chândrâyaṇa* &c., "Study"—the study of the sciences dealing with emancipation, or the repitition of the *Praṇava*. "Devotion to the Lord"—the offering of all actions to the supreme and venerable. "Seated on the bed or wandering on the road, if he is calm on having his doubts and misgivings removed, and looking upon the destruction of the seed of metempsychosis,—such a one would be the eternally emancipated, the experiencer of the joys of immortality." In this connection it has been declared: "Thence the right knowledge of the retrogade sentience, and the removal of obstacles" (*Yoga-sutra.* I-29).

Of these, when Restraints and Penances—

Sutra (33):—are obstructed by questionables, the constant pondering of the opposites (is necessary).

Com:—When the Brâhmaṇa is obsessed by the questionables,—harmfulness and the rest (to be described in the next aphorism,—such as "I will kill my malefactor," "I shall tell an untruth," "I shall take hold of his property," "I will be vulgar with his wife," "I will be master of his holdings,"—he becomes obstructed by the glaring fever of questionables leading to evil ways, the neophyte is to ponder over the opposites thereof—*i. e.*, he should think thus: Boiled in the terrific fire of metempsychosis I have taken refuge in the virtues of yoga, through charity and love towards all beings; so if I revert to the questionable paths after having once given them up, then I would be acting like a miserable cur—reverting to the relinquished, just as the dog licks up the vomitted food. The same process is to be applied to the other aphorisms as well (*i. e.*, those treating of purification and the rest).

Sutra (34):—The questionables are slaughter (harmfulness) and the rest;—"(and whether these are) done, caused to be done, or approved of (abetted); (whether) preceded by (caused by) covetousness, anger or delusion; (whether) slight, moderate or excessive,—they (always) have pain and ignorance for their endless fruits"—thus is the pondering upon (their) opposites.

Com :—Slaughter is threefold, being either done, caused to be done, or abetted,—each of these again is three fold : (1) caused by convetousness *i. e*, for the sake of the flesh or the skin ; (2) by anger—*i. e.*, thinking the object to be one's injuror; (3) by delusion—*i. e.*, thinking that virtue will result therefrom (as the slaughter in sacrifices). Covetousness anger and delusion too are three fold : being slight moderate or excessive. Thus there are 27 forms of slaughter. The *slight* &c., again are each threefold : the slight, the moderate-slight and the excessive-slight ; and again the slight-moderate, the moderate-moderate, the excessive-moderate ; and lastly the slight-excessive, the moderate-excessive, and the excessive–excessive. Thus slaughter becomes, eightyone-fold. Again in accordance with decision, doubt and collectivity (1) when it is decided that fish is to be killed ((2) when it is doubtful whether the fish or the goat is to be killed ; and (3) when both of them are to be killed,) it becom es innumerable, because of the innumerability of living beings. The same divisions are to be applied to untruth and the rest also.

"These questionables have pain and ignorance for their endless fruits"—thus is to be the pondering upon their opposites.—e. g., the killer first of all cripples the powers of the animal to be slaughtered (by binding it fast to some pole &c.,) then gives it pain by letting fall some weapon, and then deprives it of its life even. Then from the crippling of its power results the crippling of the powers of the killer's accoutrements (or accessories), both animate (wife &c.) and inanimate (bed, food &c.) ; from the animals pain results his own misery in hell, and during future brute existence (the necessary consequence of slaughter) ; and the loss of life leads to his continuous existence on the brink of death (on account of some incurable disease) (during which state), though wishing to be dead, he still breathes, on account of there being a fixed time for the fruition of pain (as death would save him from much pain, so he is allowed to live, but only in order that he may undergo all the pain due to him on account of the the tortures he administered to the animal he slaughtered.) If by some virtuous deed, the taint of slaughter was washed off, then having gained pleasure (recovery from the malady), he would have his life cut short. As far as possible the above is to be applied to the cases of falsehood and the rest also. Thus then, pondering over the above necessary undesirable consequence of the questionables, one ought never to set his heart upon them. The questionables are to be avoided by the pondering upon their opposites.

When these questionables shall have become non-procreative, then the perfection of the Yogi resulting therefrom would imply his occult powers, such as—

Sutra (35):—Non-slaughter being confirmed, there is suspension of hostility in his vicinity.

Com :—In his vicinity all living beings give up their everlasting hostilities.

Sutra (36):—Veracity being confirmed, there is the asylum of fruits of actions.

Com :—(The veracious Yogi saying) "be virtuous," the man (spoken to) becomes virtuous ; (and on his saying) a "Attain to heaven" he attains to it ;—thus his words become immediately effective.

Sutra (37):—Abstinence from theft being confirmed, all jewels approach him.

Com :—Jewels from all sides pour down upon him.

Sutra (38) :—Continence being confirmed, the attainment of vigour—

Com :—By the attainment of this, the Yogi raises to perfection the irrepressible qualities (the powers); and becoming perfected he is able to infuse wisdom into his disciples.

Sutra (39) :—Non-covetousness being confirmed, knowledge of the how and wherefore of births.

Com :—Supply "accrue to him." "Who was I? How was I? What is this (birth)? How is this? What shall I be? How shall I be?"—Such longings after knowing all about his past, present and future births, become by themselves satisfied.

Now we speak with regard to the Observances.

Sutra (40) :—From purity, disgust for one's own body and non-intercourse with others.

Com:—Being disgusted with his body the Yogi begins purifications; but finding the body to be full of discrepancies, he loses all attachment thereto, and thus becomes "self-controlled" (*Yati*). And further (there is) "non-intercourse with others"—looking upon the nature of the body, and desiring to give up his own body on account of not finding it purified even on being washed with clay and water,—how can such a one have intercourse with the extremely dirty bodies of others?

And also

Sutra (41) :—Purity, complacency, concentration, subjugation of the senses, and fitness for communion with the Spirit—(all accruing) to the thinking principle (*Lit.* Goodness).

Com :—From purification results the "purity" of the thinking principle (mind), thence its complacency, thence its concentration, thence its subjugation of the senses, and finally its fitness for spiritual communion,—all these result from the confirmation of purity.

Sutra (42) :—From contentment, superlative felicity.

Com :—As has been declared : "Whatever constitutes the desirable pleasure in this world, and whatever great pleasure there is in heaven,—all these do not compare with the sixteenth part of the felicity attendant upon the suppression of desires."

Sutra (43) :—From penance, after the decay of impurities, the occult powers of the body and the senses.

Com :—As soon as penance is accomplished, it destroys the enveloping impurity ; and from the removal of this enveloping impurity result the occult powers of the body (Buoyancy and the rest) and of the senses (hearing and seeing at great distances &c.)

Sutra (44) :—From study, communion with the desired deity.

Com :—To one given to study, the Gods, the sages and the perfectons, all become perceptible, and are ready for his actions.

Sutra (45) :—From devotion to the Lord, the accomplishment of meditation.

Com :—Meditation is accomplished for one who has offered up all his connections with the Lord ; and by this accomplishment, he rightly knows all that is good for him, in other places, in other bodies and at other time ; thence his consciousness perceives all things rightly.

Restraints and observances, together with the attendant powers, have been described ; we now speak of Posture of the rest.

Sutra (46) :—Posture is that which is steady and easy.

Com:—And there are : the (1) *Padmásana* (lotus) (2) *Veerásana* (heroic), (3) *Bhadrásana* (decent), (4) *Svastikásana* (like the mystic sign) (5) *Dandásana* (staff), (6) *Sopaśrayásana* (supported) (7) *Paryankásana* (bedstead), (8) *Kraunchanishadasana* (seated heron), (9) *Hastanishádásana* (seated elephant), (10) *Ushtranishadasana* (seated camel), (11) *Samasansthanasana* (evenly balanced), (12) *Sthirasukhásana* (the steady and pleasant) *i. e.*, in accordance with one's pleasure, and so forth.

Note.—For the definitions of these postures, the reader is referred to the *Hatha-yoga-pradipika*."

Sutra (47) :—By slackening of effort, and the contemplation of the infinite.

Com:—"Supply—"it (posture) is accomplished." On the cessation of effort, posture is accomplished; and there is no quivering of the body. Or, the mind contemplating on the Infinite accomplishes Posture.

***Sutra* (48):—Thence, Non-Embarrasment by the pairs (of opposites).**

Com:—By the accomplishment posture, the Yogi is not embarrased by the pairs of opposites—such as heat and cold &c.

***Sutra* (49):—Thereupon, the Regulation of Breath,—the controlling of the course of inspiration and expiration.**

Com:—On the accomplishment of posture, results the Regulation of Breath, which consists in the interruption (stoppage) in the course of inspiration (the inhaling of air) and expiration (the exhaling of the inhaled air).

And that again

***Sutra* (50):—is an external, internal or stationary function,—regulated by place, time and number,—protracted or subtile (long or short).**

Com:—The interruption, preceded by expiration, is external; and that again, preceded by in inspiration, is internal; the absence of both is the third, the stationary function, attainable by a single effort; just as a drop of water placed on a heated stone—slab, becomes shrivelled from all sides, so is the absence of the two (inspiration and expiration).

All these three are "regulated by place",—"This particular place is its object"; "regulated by time"—as characterised by the measures of time; "regulated of number",—the first stroke is to consist of so many inspirations and expirations; in the same manner the second stroke of the overpowered (breath) is to consist of so many; in the same manner the third, so the slight, so the moderate, so the excessive,—such is the regulation by number. And this regulation of Breath when practised, is protracted or subtile (long or short).

Sutra (51) :—The fourth is dependent on the recognition of the outer and inner spheres.

Com :—The "outer sphere" regulated by place, time and number being passed over, so also the inner sphere regulated in the same manner, being passed over,—both being protracted as well as subtile—that which is preceded by these, and consists of the subjugation of the stages in the social stoppage of then two,—is the fourth kind of Regulation of Breath. The third is the interruption untouched by any object, no sooner began than regulated by place, time and number,—being protracted and subtile; and the fourth is the interruption preceded by the indication of the first two, brought forth by the subjugation of the stages, through the recognition of the objects of exhalation and inhalation; such is the difference between the 3rd and 4th (the third is not preceded by the cognition of any object, and is brought about by a single effort, whereas the fourth is preceded by the recognition of objects and is only amenable to long continued effort).

Note :—The 1st the *External*, the Exhalation is the Réchaka.
The 2nd the *Internal*, Inhalation—is the Pûraka.
The 3rd is the Kumbhaka 1st kind.
and 4th Do. 2nd kind.

Sutra (52) :—Then is destroyed the envelope of light.

Com :—Of the Yogi practising the regulation of breath, the action enveloping right knowledge is destroyed. This is thus described—"The net of great delusion enveloping the illuminative goodness, turns it towards evil deeds." This light-enveloping and birth-causing action of the Yogi is attenuated by the practice of the regulation of breath, and is decaying every moment. As has been declared : "There is no penance above the regulation of breath ; because there-from results the removal of impurities and the illumination of knowledge."

And also,

Sutra (53) :—the fitness of the mind for concentration.

Com :—This also results from regulation of breath alone, in accordance with the aphorism : "Or by the expulsion and retention of breath"—(*Yoga-Sutra*—I-34.)

Now what is Abstraction ?

Sutra (54) :—Abstraction is the assumption, as it were, by the senses of the original nature of the mind, from want of application to their (respective) objects.

Com :—On the absence of application to their respective objects, results the "assumption, as it were, of the original nature of the mind"—that is to say, on the suppression of the mind, the senses also becoming suppressed, do not stand in need of any other means, like the control of other senses (*i.e.*, one sense being suppressed by a certain means, the subjugation of the other senses stands in need of other means ;)

but on the suppression of the mind, that of the senses follows directly. Just as the bees fly along with the chief of the black bees, and rest after he has rested, so on the suppression of the mind, the senses become subjugated—and this constitutes Abstraction.

Sutra (55) :—Thence the complete subjugation of the senses.

Com :—"The subjugation of the senses consists in the non-hankering after the various sensuous objects, sound and the rest"--so say some. Hankerling is attachment, that which alienates the agent from his advancement. The applications not contradictory (to scripture) is allowable (so this application, free from any that is contradictory to the scrupture, constitutes subjugation, according to others). The optional communion with objects (is subjugation)—say others. (That is, the senses turning towards and touching objects only when desired by the agent). Others again assert the subjugation of the senses to consist in perception of sound and the rest, free from pleasure and pain, through the absence of attachment and aversion. It is total non-perception (absence of sensation) due to concentration—says Jaig-ishavya. Thence (from abstraction) follows this highest form of subjugation—*viz.*, suppression of the mind, the senses being subjugated it does not, as in the case of subjugation of the senses, stand in need of any other means due to any effort of the Yogi.

SECTION III.

OF THE OCCULT POWERS.

The five outer means having been described, the author now proceeds to explain Concentration.

Sutra (1) :—**Concentration is the fixing of the mind to a certain locality.**

Com :—It is the fixing of the mind solely through its function, on the navel, the lotus of the heart, the light in the brain, the tip of the nose, and the tip of the tongue &c., or on external objects.

Sutra (2) :—**Contemplation consists in the uninterrupted current of cognition thereof.**

Com:—*i e.,* the uniform flow in that place of the cognition reposing in the object contemplated. That is to say, contemplation is untouched by any other cognition.

Note :—"In that place" *i.e.,* in the places mentioned in the preceding aphorism.

Sutra (3) :—**The same, enlightening the object alone, and devoid of its own identity as it were, is Meditation.**

Com:—When Contemplation is conscious of the form of the object, and appears as if devoid of its own character of consciousness, then on account of its being infused with the character of the contemplated object, it becomes *meditation.*

Note : (1) "*On account of &c.*"—This is added in anticipation of the objection that becoming devoid of its own character, it would lose its enlightening power.

These three Concentration, Contemplation and Meditation together constitute *Sanyama* :

Sutra (4) :—The three together constitute *Sanyama.*

Com:—The three means having a single object, are called *Sanyama,* which thus is the technical name for the three taken collectively.

Sutra (5) :—From success therein results the lucidity of consciousness.

Com:—By mastering *Sanyama,* results the lucidity of meditative consciousness. As *Sanyama* becomes established so does meditative consciousness become lucid.

Sutra (6) :—It is applied by stages.

Com :—Sanyama is applied to another stage only when it has mastered the preceding one. *Sanyama* can never attain to the final (highest) stage, by jumping over the intermediate stages, without conquering these latter. (The condition of the perceived object being the lowest stage, that of the organ of perception the intermediate stage, and that of the perceiver, the final stage). And without its attaining to the highest stage, whence the lucidity of consciousness? For one who has through divine favour conquered the following stages, it is not necessary to practise *Sanyama* with regard to the preceding ones. Why? Because the objects of this latter will have already been cognised through the former. In the knowledge of the order of the stages—that this stage preceded that—yoga is the only guide. Why? Because it has been declared: "Yoga is to be recognised by yoga; from yoga does yoga proceed; one who is not confused by yoga, he ever delights in yoga."

Sutra (7) :—The three are more intimate (directly effective) than the former ones.

Com:—The three-Concentration, Contemplation and Meditation—are more directly effective in accomplishing concrete meditation, than the former ones, Restraint and the rest.

Notes : "Intimate"—"Antaranga"—*i. e.*, more closely related *i. e.*, directly effective.

Sutra (8) :—It is still foreign to the seedless. (Abstract).

Com:—The preceding intimate triad of means is foreign to the seedless (abstract) meditation; Why ? Because Abstract meditation appears only when the three are absent.

Sutra (9) :—Suppressive (or interceptive) modification is the conjunction of the mind with the moment of suppression, on the overthrow and prevalence of the distractive (waking) and suppressive impressions (respectively).

Com:—The distractive impressions being the properties (material effects) of the mind, are not identical with cognition, and as such are not suppressed by the suppression of the cognition (in fact, they always outlive the cognitions of which they are the impressions; it is only the material cause whose suppression causes that of the effect also) ; the suppressive impressions also are properties of the mind; —the (respective) "overthrow and prevalence" of these—*i. e.*, when the distractive impressions are wasting, and the suppressive impression gaining ground, then the moment of suppression conjoins with the mind. Thus the constant change of impressions, occurring in the mind is suppressive modification. And then the mind has only the impressions left behind,—as has been explained under suppressive (abstract) Meditation (I. 18).

Notes: (1)—Dr. Mitra construes as *pratyanirodhena niruddhah,* and takes it with the following *chittadharmah.* But the translation follows the interpretation of Vachaspati Misra, who thus introduces the passage: "The impressions caused by distractive cognitions (*i.e.*, those of the waking state) would cease on the cessation of the waking state, and as such for its cessation we would not stand in need of the suppressive modification." The sense of the reply is given in parenthesis above.

Sutra **(10) :—Its flow becomes tranquil from residual habit.**

Com :—From suppressive residua results the tranquil flow of the mind, which depends on the expertness in the practice of suppressive residua. When those residua become dulled, the residua having suppression for their property are overthrown by those whose property is distraction.

Sutra **(11) :—The destruction and enlivenment (respectively) of the multifunctionality and concentration of the mind is (its) *meditative* modification.**

Com :—Multifuctionality is a property of the mind, and so is Concentration ; the meaning is that there is destruction or decay of multifuctionality and enlivenment or rise of Concentration ; both of these are correlated to the mind which holds them as its properties. Thus this mind, co-rrelated to its co-natural (or identical) properties,—the aforesaid decay and rise,—becomes collected or pacified; and this is its "meditative modification."

Sutra **(12) :—Then again, the concentrative modification of the mind is that in which both the reppressed and the revived are equally recognised.**

Com:—Of one whose mind is pacified, the foregoing cognition is the 'reppressed,' and the following one similar thereto is the 'revived'; and the meditative mind, correlated to the two is the same (i. e., collected or concentrated). Thus this is the 'concentrative modification' of the mind to which the cognitions are related as its properties.

Sutra (13) :—This also explains the modifications of property, time and condition, in the elementary substances and the sense-organs.

Com:—"This"—*i.e.*, the aforesaid modifications of the mind —explains the modifications in the elementary substances and the sense-organs,—of property, time and condition.

Of these the "modification of property" consists in the reppression and rise of the distractive and suppressive properties in the object having those properties (*i.e.*, in their respective causes).

The "modification of time" is the suppression of its threefold character—*i.e.*, characterised by the three limitations (of time). This suppression, first of all relinquishing the limitation of *futurity*, and not passing over its *property-ness*, becomes conjoined with the limitation of the *present*, wherein it becomes manifested in its true colour. This is its second limitation; nor is this disjoined from the limitation of the *past* and *future*. Similarly, distraction (the waking state), of threefold character—*i.e.*, characterised by the three limitations (of time),—relinquishing the limitation of the *present*, and not passing over its property-ness, becomes conjoined with the limitation of the *past*;—this is its third limitation; nor is this disjoined from the limitations of the *present* and the *future*. Similarly again, distraction becoming accomplished, and (thereby) relinquishing its limitation of *futurity*, and not passing over its property-ness, becomes related to the limitation of the *present*, wherein its manifesting in its true colours, begins its operations. This is its second limitation; nor does it get free from the limitations of the past and the future. So again suppression, and also distraction.

In the same manner, the "modification of condition"—(is that) wherein, during the moments of suppression, the suppressive residua are strengthened, and the distractive residua are weakened. This is the modification of the condition of the properties.

Among these, the modification of the object having the properties, is by means of these properties; that of the properties is by means of the limitations; and lastly that of the limitations by means of the conditions.

Thus the function of the attributes does not even for a moment exist without the modifications of property, time and condition (*i. e.*, it is constantly producing modifications); because the function of the attributes is ever mobile; and the cause of operation has been said to be the subordinate character of the attributes.

Thus in the elementary substances and the sense-organs, owing to the distinction between the property and the object having it, there are three kinds of modifications. In reality however, the modification is one only. Because the property is only a form of the object possessing it; and as such the above is only the consideration of certain modifications of the object, through the properties (*i. e.*, through the modifications of the properties). Hence, during the past, present and future states, what becomes of the property present in the object (which holds it) is only a change in its position (form), and not any change of the (constitutent) matter.

As for example, to a golden vessel on being broken, and made to undergo a change, the only change that happens is that of form, and not that of the gold itself.

Says another (the Bauddha holding the complete identity of the property and the object possessing it): "The object is nothing more than the property, in as much as it does not go beyond the former material; for if the object continued its existence through the various modifications (of the property), then it would in reality become unchangeable."

(To this we make the following reply:)—There is no harm in this. Why? Because, we do not assert its absoluteness. Thus all the three worlds recede from manifestation (*i.e.*, recede from *present* activity and become the *past*), simply because of the denial of the (unchangeable) eternity (of mundane objects). And though receded (become past), still it exists, because of the denial of its destruction; its minuteness is due to its correlation (*i.e.*, resolution into its cause); and from its minuteness results imperceptibility. The property, having the modification of time, existing in the various limitations (*lakshaṇa*, of time), becoming *past*, and thus becoming conjoined with the limitation of the *past*, is not disjoined from the limitations of the *present* and the *future*; similarly the *future*, joined to the limitation of the *future*, is not disjoined from those of the *past* and *present*; and lastly the *present*, joined to the limitation of the *present*, is not disjoined from those of the *past* and the *future*. (That is to say every individual limitation is accompained by the other two) Just as, because a man is attached to a certain woman, it does not follow that he has an aversion for other women.

Here, in the modification of time (limitation), all the limitations occuring together, there would result an admixture of limitations. If this is urged as an objection, then we make the following reply: The character of the property having been established, we have to describe its different limitations; for certainly its special character belongs to the property not only at the present time, (but it has the same character even in the past and the future). For otherwise the mind would not have attachment for its property, because attachment does not exist when there is anger. And further, the simultaneous relation of any individual with the three limitations, is not possible; by degrees however there is the manifestation of it, by means of its manifesting cause. As has been declared: "The excessive manifestation, of forms and those of functions are opposed to one another, but the genuine ones act in consort with the excessive manifestations" (vide this quotation under II—15). Therefore, there can no admixture (as has been urged by the objector).

As from the activity of attachment with regard to a certain object, it is not inferred that it does not exist anywhere else,—the fact being that it is related to the latter too, in a general way,—so the same is the case with limitation (*lakshaṇa*): It is the property, and not the object possessing the property, that has the three limitations: The properties, manifested (*present*) as well as well as unmanifested, (*past and future*), attaining to the various conditions (of weakness, strength and the like), are said to have been changed—but this change is only in (condition), not in matter. Just as a single line in the place of hundreds, becomes hundred, in the place of tens a ten, and in the place of units a unit; and again, as a single woman is called mother, daughter and mother-in-law (according to circumstances, the woman remaining the same).

Against the theory of the "modification of conditions," some people have raised the objection that in that case there would be an unchangeable eternality (for objects and their properties); because, a property is said to be in the *future* when, being removed from the range of the activity of the limitation, it does not carry out its own operations; when it carries on its operations, it is said to be in the *present*, and lastly, when it has ceased after having operated, it is said to be in the *past*.--And thus we find that the limitations and the conditions of the properties and the objects having them are unchangeably eternal. This is the objection urged.

(We reply):—This is not a sound objection; because though the object having an attribute is eternal, yet there is quite a variety of the forms of the suppression (or over-throw) of the attributes themselves; just as the destructible (suppressible), agglomeration (earth and the rest) is a mere property of the indestructible (irrepressible) sound, odour &c. (rudimentary elements); similarly the reppressible *mergent* (Linga, the *Buddhi*) is a mere property of the irrepressible (Attributes) Goodness and the rest. Thus their modification is attributed to these (*i. e.*, the properties *Buddhi*, Earth &c). Here we have the following instance: The object clay, acquiring a property other than that of a lump, becomes modified by the property, into the form of a jar; and this form of the jar, relinquishing the future limitation, attains to the present one, and thus becomes modified by limitation; and lastly, the jar momentarily becoming new and old, acquires the modification of condition. The change of the properties of an object is a condition; and the change in the limitation of the property is also a condition; thus the change in matter is only one (*i.e*, the modification of condition); but this has been shown in its various divisions (*i. e.*, though there is in fact only one modification, that of condition, still the other two—that of property and limitation have been explained separately, though really being the only particular forms of that of condition alone). The same consideration is to be applied to all other objects.

All these modifications of property and limitation and condition never outgrowing the form of the object, the modification is one alone, and this includes all the other particular ones.

Now what do you mean by "modification"? Modification consists in the appearance of fresh properties for a certain object, following on the cessation (or reppression) of the former ones.

Notes: (1) "*It becomes manifested in its true colour*"—The suppression, that was future ere this, becomes the present now; the one kind of suppression does not cease to be suppress ion in order to make room for the other suppression.

(2) "*Subordinate character of the attributes.*" We find in daily life the servants always acting for their master; similarly the fact of goodness &c. being of the same subordinate nature (like the servant), accounts for their constant activity.

(3) "*And not any change of the constituent matter.*" because if the change took place in the matter, then the object undergoing a momentary change, would never be recognised as the same.

(4) "*If the object continued its existence through the various modifications &c.*" If the object were so, then it would be equally related to the past and the future as well, and thus would result its eternality and unchangeableness, like that of the sentient faculty; and certainly this will not be palatable to the Bauddha objector either.

(5) "*We do not assert its absoluteness.*" If like that of sentient faculty we also asserted the absolute eternality of the objects, then would the objection apply to us; as it is however, we do not make any such assertion. In fact we go so far as to assert the cessation of the activity of all the three worlds, to say nothing of particular objects.

(6) "*Denial of its destruction,*"—The reasoning is this:— What is non-existent never operates, as sky-flowers; the three worlds however do operate; and as such they can never be said to be non-existent. Thus though we deny their absolute eternality, yet as they are never entirely destroyed, this modified eternality may be asserted of them.

(7) "*Minuteness.*" In anticipation of the objection that the object being never destroyed, wherefore do we not perceive objects of the

past ?—the reply is that their imperceptibility is due to their having been resolved into their respective causes.

(8) "*Otherwise, the mind would not have attachment* &c. It is only after anger has passed off that the mind is found to have attachment; and thus if attachment did not latently exist there in its future state, whence its later appearance ? For certainly anything that is non-existent can never be brought into existence.

(9) "*Though the object having an attribute is eternal &c.*" Though the object (Purusha) as well as the attributes (goodness &c.) are equally constant entities, still the latter being amenable to periodical appearance and reppression, and as such having modifications, can not be said to be unchangeably (absolutely) eternal. The sentient faculty is not so; and hence it is said to be absolutely eternal.

Among these—

Sutra (14) :—The subject is that which is correlated to the properties of tranquility, activity, and latency (indescribability).

Com :—The property is only the faculty of the subject, characterised by capability; and its existence being inferred from the variety of its effects, it is found to be manifold with regard to the one subject.

Of these the present (active) property, its own activity, becomes differentiated from the other properties,—the tranquil (past) and the latent (future) ones. When however it is correlated only in a general form, then consisting merely of the form of the subject, wherefrom should it differentiate? Thus the properties of the subject are three—the tranquil, the active and the latent. Of these the *tranquil* are those that have receded after having done their work; those that are operating are the *active*; both of these precede the future; the past precedes the present. Wherefore are not the present ones said to precede the past ones? Because among these two there is no order of precedence; as the order of precedence that we find between the past and the future is not found in the case of the past with regard to the present. Therefore there is nothing that precedes the past. For this reason the future precedes the present (this in accordance with the theory of the continued existence of the effect latent in the cause, before its manifestation).

Now which are the *latent* ones? (Reply) Everything having the character of everything. With regard to this it is declared : (3) "Among the immovable objects we find the universality of the effects in the form of the different tastes, belonging to Water and Earth; similarly of the immovables with regard to the movable, and *vice versa*" Thus the genus not being suppressed (or else the various effects would not be recognised), everything has the nature of everything. Though this is so, yet their manifestation is not simultaneous, because of the manifestation being conditioned by place, time, and form. That which is correlated to these manifested and unmanifested properties, and which has both the general (belonging to the subject) and the special character (of the property),—such a correlative is the subject. One (the Yogâchâra) however who asserts the property to be unconnected (with anything else, because he denies the existence of any subject other than the properties of cognition and the like), for him there would be no experience. Why? Because the actions performed by a certain idea (or cognition) cannot transfer its effect to the other idea (for according to these theorists there is nothing except ideas, and these are momentary); and again there could be no memory of the action; for an object seen by one (idea) cannot be remembered by another. Because of the recognition of objects (previously perceived), there must be a subject correlative (to the various modifications of the object), which is recognised as the same, after its properties have undergone a change. Therefore it cannot be rightly held that all that exists is mere unconnected property.

Notes (1) "*Existence being inferred &c*"—The sense is that of a single subject the property of the form of capability is seen to be manifold—the capability lying latent in its cause.

(2) "*When however it is correlated &c.*" This addition establishes the differentiation of the unmanifested cause.

(3) "*Among the immovable objects &c*":—In the joint modifications of Earth and Water—the trees and the like—we find the various kinds of taste &c.; that of the immovable in the movable we find in the modifications of air, water &c., in the animal body; that of the movable in the immovable—in the enlarging of the pomegranate by being sprinkled with blood.

Sutra (15).—The change of order is the cause of the versatility (or changeableness) of modifications.

Com:—"The modification of one subject should be one only"—this being urged, (we reply) that the change of order can be the cause of the versatility of the modifications. As for instance, the proper order is—*dust* of clay, *lump* of clay, the jar-clay, the clay of the broken jar, and the clay of the small pieces. The proper order is the mention of the following property next to the one that precedes it—*e.g.*, the lump disappearing, the jar appears—such is the order of the modification of property. The order of the modification of limitation—as the present state of the jar after its future, the past state of the lump after its present; as for the past, there is no order because when there is succession, then only can there be an order; but there is no succession of the past; therefore there is order only of the first two limitations (the present and the future). Similarly the order of the modification of condition—*e.g.*, the oldness of the jar after its newness; and this oldness being manifested by the order of the series of moments, attains to final manifestation. This is the third modification, above those of the property and its limitation.

These various orders, acquiring their form on the differentiation of the subject and the property,—certain properties also become subjects with reference to certain other properties. When however there is the idea of identity (of the property) in the subject,—and thus that property being mentioned thereby (*i.e.*, by naming the subject),—then the order appears to be one only. Of the mind, the properties are two-fold—the perceived and the unperceived; of these the former are the cognitions, and the latter, the objects themselves. These, having their objective character got at by means of inference are seven: (1) suppression (the state of absolute meditation inferred from the disappearence of all residua) (2) Virtue (and vice, inferred from the resulting pleasure and pain), (3) Residual Impressions (inferred from memory), (4) Modification (inferred from the mobility of the attributes), (5) Life (the effort to live inferred from breathing), (6) Movements (action inferred from the activity of the various senses), and (7) Capability or Power (the latent condition of the effects, existing in their causes).—these are the seven properties of the mind, devoid of perception.

Henceforward begins the consideration of the objects of *sanyama*, for the accomplishment of the ends of the yogi equipped with all the accessories.

Sutra (16).—The knowledge of the past and future (is acquired) through *sanyama* over the three modifications.

Com:—From *sanyama* over the modifications of property, time and condition, accrues to the yogi the knowledge of the past and the future. Sanyama has been defined as consisting in concentration, contemplation and meditation taken together. Hence the three modifications being perceived, the yogi accomplishes the knowledge of the past and future related thereto.

Sutra (17).—The word, the objected denoted by it and its idea are commingled with one another, on account of their being mistaken for one another; hence by *sanyama* over the distinct provinces of each of these, (arises) the comprehension of the cry of all creatures.

Com :—The organ of speech has its purpose solely with the letter pronounced ; the organ of hearing has the modification of sound for its object ; and the word finally is perceptible through the apprehension of the letters taken collectively. The letters, not coming in simultaneously, and hence not aided by one another, do not affect the word; and as such not giving rise to (any idea), but each of them appearing and disappearing by turns—are severally said to be incapable of forming the word. Every one of the letters, forming a word, —capable of a host of denotations (when taken severally), yet when correlated with the accompanying letters, and hence becoming manifold, become so placed that each of them is confined to the particular word by the other [*i.e.*, the single letter *ga* has the capability of denoting *gau, gaṇa, gaura* &c., so long as it is taken by itself; but as soon as the letter *ga* is joined with the letters *au*, &c., it becomes manifold ; and each of the two letters serves to confine the other to the particular word in question. Thus (we see that) the various letters, depending on the order of succession become characterised by the convention of meaning, and though capable of all sorts denotations, yet becoming subordinated to the *ga* and the *au*, denote the particular object with the dewlap &c. (*i.e.* the cow). Thus the cognition of the unity of these,—

as characterised by conventional meaning, and having the order of utterance drawn together (*i.e.* considered collectively) —is said to be the denotative name for the object named. Thus a single word,—being the object of a single cognition, being put forth by a single effort, devoid of any distinction (between the letters) (and hence also) of the order and of letters, belonging to consciousness, brought forth by the action of the last letter (as helped by the impressions left in the memory, of the preceding ones),—is cognised as a real entity by the popular mind correlated with the impressions of everlasting linguistic usage, by means of the letters, uttered with a view to express the objects to others, and heard by the listener. And the disintegration of this word (into its letters) is due to the notion of convention,—(the popular idea being that) the denotator of the object is such and such a particular arrangement of so many letters.

Convention is a form of *Remembrance* consisting in the idea of the mutual identity between the word and what is denoted by it: that is convention is of this form:—the *word* is the *meaning* and the *meaning* is the *word* (an idea of identity).

Thus then; these three–the word, the object denoted by it and the idea,–become commingled on account of being mistaken for another—'cow' the word, 'cow' the object, 'cow' the idea; and one who knows the distinction of these, knows everything. Every word has the force of a sentence: the word 'tree' implies its existence; for certainly existence cannot be denied to any object. Similarly there is no action without the means; so the word "cooks" implies all the agencies pertaining to it; the further mention of the agent, the object and the instruments (Chaitra, the rice and fire) being made only in order to specify these; and further we find single words used for sentences—the word "*śrotriya*" for "studies the Vedas," the word "lives" for "holds life." In a sentence, there is an expression of the meanings of words, (thus there being the expression of the meaning of a sentence in a word, and that of the meaning of the word in a sentence, there is a confusion and) the word is to be broken up (into its constituent parts) and then explained as to which part of it expresses the verb, and which the nominative (as the word *'srotriya* is broken up into "*one* (nominative) who *studies* (verb) the *Vedas* (accusative). Or otherwise, in the case of *aśvah* (meaning by itself, both *horse* and *thòu breathedst*) and *ajâpayah* (*=the milk of the she—goat,* and also, *thou hast suppressed*), there being a confusion of the name and the verb (as shown by the two meanings of each), how could these be explained either with regard to the verb (if it were taken as a name) or to the nominative (in case it were taken as a verb)? the distinct province of these word, meaning and idea—*e.g.*, "the house is *whitening*"—the word signifying the verb (*śvéta*); and "the house is white"—here the word (*śvéta*) signifies the noun (so much for the word); (secondly) its meaning is that consisting in the verb or in the noun; and (thirdly) the idea is that which apprehends the aforesaid meanings. Why ? Because in convention the idea has only one form, being based on the identity of the signification—"this is that,"—the "white object" being the object of the word as well as of the idea. [That is to say, in the above example the idea is that of the house in front *being a white one,* whatever may be the words in which the idea is expressed]. And this object under its modifications is accompanied neither by the word, nor by the idea. Similarly the word and the idea do not accompany each other. The consciousness of the distinct province of each being in the form—'the word is different from the meaning which again is different from the idea.'

From the *Sañyama* over this distinction, accurues to the Yogi, the comprehension of the cry of all creatures.

(Notes : (1) " *In a sentence there is &c.*"—This is said in anticipation of the objection: "If the word is capable of expressing the mean-

ing of a sentence, why should there be a sentence at all?" The sense of the reply is that the use of a single word without any verb &c., is very often ambiguous, hence the necessity of the sentence.

Sutra (18): By the mental presentation of the impressions, the knowledge of previous births.

Com:—Impressions are of two kinds...(1) Those in the form of the residual longings, the cause of memory and the afflictions, and (2) those in the form of virtue and vice, leading to fruition. Both of these kinds, accomplished in the former birth, are the properties of the mind, imperceptible, like modification, movement, suppression, power, life (the properties of the mind spoken of above, III, 15). The *Sanyama* over these is capable of rendering the impressions apparent; nor is such presentation possible without a cognition of their time, place and cause (of the previous birth). Thus the knowledge of the previous birth accrues to the yogi through the mental presentation of the impressions. In the case of others too there is a similar knowledge of another's birth, following on the mental presentation of their impressions. In connection with this we have a story:—Discriminative knowledge accrued to the revered Jaigîshavya, possessing, through the mental presentation of the impressions, a knowledge of the orderly modification of his birth extending over ten *Pralayic* creations. The revered Âvatya, thus spoke to him: "Through ten *Kalpic* creations having your consciousness unrepressed, you must have come across the pains due to birth in a hellish or a brutish womb; and being born again and again among men and the gods, which of the two, pleasure and pain, did you find in a greater amount?" Jaigîshavya thus replied: "I, having my consciousness unrepressed through ten cycles, and coming across the pain due to hellish and bestial births, and being born again and again among gods and men, whatever I experienced, all I think to be solely pain." Says the revered Âvatya. "This unsurpassed pleasure of contentment consisting in mastery over Nature that thou hast...dostthou include this also under pain?" Replied the revered Jaigîshavya: "This pleasure of contentment is excellent as compared with sensuous pleasure; in comparison with isolation however, this also is pain. Because this pleasure of contentment is a property of Buddhi, and as such abounds in the three attributes; and all consciousness partaking of the three attributes, has been put under the head of 'what should be avoided.' Then, contentment is said to be pleasure because the strings of desire being of the nature of pain, on the removal of these, there is unrestricted pleasure.

Sutra (19):—With reference to cognition, the knowledge of another's mind.

Com:—From the *Sanyama* over cognition—*i.e.* from the mental presentation of the cognition (of others), results the knowledge of other's minds.

Sutra (20):—But not along with its object, that not being the object.

Com:—The Yogi knows the mind of another, as attached to something; but he does not know that "it is attached to that particular object." Because that which is the object of another's mind, is not the object of the Yogi's mind; it is only another's cognition (or mind) that is made the object of the mind of the Yogi.

Notes:—(1) This aphorism is explained by Vijnâna Bhikshu as a part of the Bhâshya.

Sutra (21):—From _Sanyama_ with reference to the shape of the body, its visibility being suspended, and thus its connection with occular light being severed,—there is disappearance.

Com:—From the *Sanyama* with regard to the shape of the body, the visibility of the shape becomes suppressed; and on this suspension, the connection of the body with the light of (other people's) eyes ceases; and thence results the disappearance of the Yogi. The disappearance of sound and the rest are to be explained in the same manner.

Sutra (22):—Karma is active and dormant; and by _Sanyama_ over this, results the knowledge of the end; as also by portents.

Com:—The Karma resulting in life is of two kinds: the *active* and the *dormant;* the *active* is similar to a wet piece of cloth spread over the ground, which dries up in a very short time; whereas the *dormant* is like the same piece of cloth tied up in a bundle, drying up in a long time; or again, the *active* is like fire in dry straw helped by the wind, burning it completely in a very short time; and the *dormant* is similar to the same fire when placed in various parts of the heap of straw, burning it in a long time. In this way the Karma "of one birth," bringing about life, is of two kinds—the *active* and the *dormant*.

By *Sanyama* over these, results the knowledge of death. "As also by portents"—portents are threefold; corporeal, elemental and celestial. Of these the 'corporeal' is that, for instance, when closing the ear one does not hear the internal sounds (produced in the stomach by breathing), or when one does not see any light on closing the eyes. Similarly the

15

'elemental' is that when one beholds the attendants of the Death-god; or when one all on a sudden sees his dead fore-fathers; and the 'celestial' is that when one suddenly beholds the heaven, or the Perfect Ones, or anything contrary to the ordinary course of events (is a portent). By these portents too one knows his end to be near at hand.

Sutra (23) :—In friendliness and the rest, (superhuman) powers.

Com :—Friendliness, mercy, and complaisance are the three Emotions or (feelings). Of those, by the feeling of friendliness towards all happy creatures, one acquires the power of friendliness. By feeling mercy for the distressed creatures he acquires the power of mercy. And by feeling a complaisance towards the righteous, he acquires the powers of complaisance. The Sanyama consisting in meditation (contemplation and concentration) proceeding from these emotions, results in such powers as have their faculties unrepressed. With regard to vicious persons one has indifference, and not any feeling;—thus in this case there is no meditation and as such no power proceeds from indifference, because of the absence of any *Sanyama* with reference to this.

Sutra (24) :—In powers, the power of the Elephant and the like.

Com :—From *Sanyama* over the power of the elephant, results elephantine power; from that over the power of *Garuda* a garuda-like power; and from that over the power of the air, the air-like power.

Sutra (25) :—From the application of the light of the (luminous) disposition, (results) the knowledge of the subtile, the intercepted and the remote.

Com :—The Extremely Luminous disposition of the mind has already been explained (in I—36). The yogi applying the light of this disposition (*i. e.*, the inner light) to the subtile intercepted or remote objects, acquires the knowledge of these (objects).

Sutra (26):—From Sanyama in the Sun, the knowledge of the worlds.

Com:—The details of this are as follows : There are seven worlds : From Avîchî to the summit of the Meru is the Earth (1). From the Meru to Dhruva (the Polar star) the Starry Region occupied by the planets, and stars (2). Above that is the fivefold Celestial Region (3)—the Mâhendra being the third of these, the fourth being the Prâjâpatya or *Maharloka* (the Luminous Region); the threefold Brâhma—the Janaloka (productive Region) Tapoloka (Region of austerities) and the *Satyaloka* (the Region of Truth). These are thus described :—" The three-regioned *Brahmaloka*, then the great Prâjâpatyaloka, then the Mâhendra Heaven, then the Sky with the stars, and lastly the Earth with the various creations." Placed above the *Avîchî*, are the six great Hellish Regions, Mahâkâla, Ambarîsha, Raurava, Mahâraurava, Kâleya Sutra and Andhatâmisra,—respectively placed in the Earth, Water, Fire, Air, Space and Darkness ; and in these are born several creatures with long leases of life therein, and who have acquired the experience of pain by their own deeds. Under these are the seven Nether Worlds : Mahâtala, Rasâtala, Atala, Sutala, Vitala, Talâtala, and Pâtâla. This our

Earth consisting of the seven continents, is the eighth ;-in the centre of which is the Land of the Mountains, the Golden Meru, whose peaks are those of silver, emerald, rock-crystal, gold, and jewels. The Southern region of the sky here is of the colour of the blue lotus through the colour of the emerald peak ; the Eastearn white, the Western clear, the Northern golden. On the Northern side of this is the *Jambu* tree, whence this particular continent is called the *Jambudwipa*. On account of the movement of the Sun, it is always touched by night and day. To the North of this are three mountains, four thousand miles high, having blue and white peaks. Within these mountain-ranges are three countries, each 72.000 Miles—Ramaṇaka, Hiraṇmaya and the Uttara Kuru. To the South are the Mountains Nishadha, Hemakuta and Hima, extending over 4,000 Miles ; within these are three countries each 72,000 miles—The Harivanśa, Kimpurūsha and the Bhârata. To the East of Meru are the Bhadrâswas extending upto the Malyavan mountains; and to the West are the Ketumâlas extending upto the Gandhamâdana mountains. In the centre is the Ilavrita. Thus are the 8,000 miles on each side of Meru surrounded by its half (wherefore Meru becomes their centre). Such is the *Jambudwipa* extending over 200,000 miles ; surrounded by the salt Ocean, twice its size. Thenceforth follow the other continents—S'âka, S'uka, Krauncha, S'âlmala, Magadha, and Pushkara—each twice the size of the other ; as also the seven Oceans—like heaps of oil-seed, interspersed with several mountains—of Sugercane-juice, Wine, Butter, Curd, Gruel, Milk, Pure Water. Thus the seven continents,—resembling so many bangles, surrounded by the seven Oceans, together with the mountains visible and invisible, reach the extent of 4,00,00,00,000 miles.

All this with its position fixed, is contained in the Egg, which is the atomic part of Matter, as the firefly in the sky. Among the nether regions, in the Oceans, and among the mountains, live Asuras, Gandharvas, Kumaras, Kimpurushas, Yakshas, Rakshasas, Bhutas, Pretas, Pisâchas, Apasmârakas, Brahmarakshasas, Küshmândas and the Vinâyakas. In the continents live the righteous gods and men. The Sumeru is the garden house of the gods. In this are the parks,—Misra, Nandana, Chaitraratha, and Sumanasa. The assembly of the gods is the Sudharmâ; their city the Sudarsana, the palace the Vaijayanta.

The planets and the stars, bound to the Pole Star, and having their motions manifested by the constant action of the wind, and placed above the Meru, keep constantly revolving. The inhabitants of the Mâhendra are the six Divine Beings—Tridashas, Agnishwâttas, Yâmyas, Tushitas, Aparinirmitavasavarti and the Parinirmitavasavarti,—all these Vrindarakas have an irresistible will, endued with the eight powers, Buoyancy and the rest, their span of life extending to a kalpa; they rejoice in sexuality, and are endowed with bodies born without sexual intercourse, have loving apsaras for their wives. In the Prâjâpatya Maharloka live the five Divine Beings—the *Kumudas*, the *Ribhavas*, *Pratardanas*, of the *Anjanabhas*, and the *Prachitabhas*. These having the great elements under their power, live in contemplation upto a thousand Kalpas. In the first, Janaloka, of Brahma, there are the four divine beings, the Brahmapurohitas, the Brahmakayikas, the Brahmamahakayikas, and the Amaras—these have command over the elements and the sense-organs. In the second, the Tapoloka, of Brahma, there are the three Divine beings—the Abhaswaras, the Mahabhaswaras, and the Satyamahabhaswaras—having command over the elements, the senses and Nature—having their span of life double of one another; all living on contemplation, their semen withheld, their knowledge unobstructed in the higher regions, and in the lower regions having the objects all unveiled to their view. In the third the Satyaloka of Brahmâ, there are four Divine Beings—the Achyutas, the Suddhanivasas, the Satyabhas, and the Sanjnasanjis. These have no houses of their own, and abiding in themselves, living one over the other, commanding Nature, live so long as the creation lasts. Of these, the Achyutas rejoice in the bliss of argumentative meditation, the Suddhanivâsa in the bliss of contemplative meditation, the Satyabhas in the contemplation of pure bliss; and the Sanjnasanjais rejoice in that of pure Egoism. These four exist in the three worlds (*i. e.* are not mukta.)

In fact all these seven worlds belong to Brahmâ. The disembodied ones and those that have been resolved into Nature however continue in the line of Emancipation and have no place in the ordinary world.

All this is to be directly perceived by the yogi, by *Sanyama* in the Sun ; as also by that in others. The Sanyama is to be practised so long as these are not perceived.

Sutra (27) :—In the moon, the knowledge of the Starry Regions.

Com: Through *Sanyama* in the moon the yogi is to know the position of the Stars.

Sutra (28) :—In the Polar Star, the knowledge of their motions.

Com :—By Sanyama in the Polar Star one is to know the motion of the stars. By Sanyama applied to the upper firmament one is to know them.

Sutra (29) :—In the circle of the navel, the knowledge of arrangement of the body.

Com :—By Sanyama in the navel-circle, one is to know the arrangement of the body. In the body there are three humours—Wind, Bile and Phlegm; and there are seven substances—skin, blood, flesh, sinews, bone, marrow and semen—these being named in order of externality (the most external being placed first).

Sutra (30):—In the throat-pit the cessation of hunger and thirst.

Com :—Below the tongue there is a thread, below which is the throat, below which is the pit, by the Sanyama of which, hunger and thirst cease to trouble the yogi.

Sutra (31):—In the *tortoise-tube*, steadiness.

Com :—Below the abovementioned pit there is a tube of the shape of a tortoise (*placed like a serpent or the alligator*), by Sanyama whereof, the yogi attains to a steady position.

Sutra (32):—In the coronal light, vision of the Perfect Ones.

Com :—Under the skull there is a hole effulgent with light—by Sanyama whereof there is vision of the Perfect Ones, wandering midway between the Earth and Heaven.

Sutra (33):—Or, from intuition (or insight), everything.

Com :—Intelligence is the Emancipator,—the forerunner of discriminative knowledge, as the Dawn is of Sunrise. On the production of intuitional insight, the yogi comes to know everything,

---

Sutra (34) :—In the heart, knowledge of mind.

Com :—In this city of Brahma (the body) there is a pit, the lotus-like house—therein results consciousness, from the Sanyama whereof, results the knowledge of mind.

Sutra (35) :—Experience is the undifferentiated conception of the attribute of goodness and the Spirit which, are quite unconnected ; (and this experience) being for another's purpose, the knowledge of the Spirit arises from the *Sanyama* on his own object.

Com :—The attribute of Sattva belonging to the Buddhi, and being of the nature of illumination, suppresses Rajas and Tamas, which are equally related to Sattva—and thus develops into the cognition of the difference of the attribute of Sattva and the Purusha. The Spirit, being essentially pure, and solely consisting of intelligence, is absolutely dissimilar to the modifying attribute of Sattva. The undifferentiated conception of these two which are absolutely unconnected, is the Soul's Experience,—all objects being presented to him. This experiential conception of the attribute of Sattva being for another's purpose, is perceptible. That which is distinct therefrom,-*i.e.* the Soul's conception consisting of pure intelligence,—by *Sanyama* over this, there arises knowledge having the Soul for its object. The Soul is not perceived by the spiritual conception constituted by the sattva of Buddhi. In fact it is the Soul itself that perceives the conception based on its own nature ; as has been declared—" Whereby is one to know the knower ? " (Brihad Upa.).

Note:—(*1*) " *The Soul is not perceived &c.*"—because it is Intelligence that perceives the insentient, not *vice versa*.

Sutra (36) :—Thence proceed intuitional cognition, audition, touch, vision, gustation and olfaction.

Com :—From intuition proceeds the cognition of the subtile, intercepted, remote, past and future objects; from audition proceeds the hearing of celestial sounds; from touch the cognition of celestial touch ; from vision the consciousness of celestial form ; from gustation, the cognisance of celestial taste, and from olfaction the cognisance of celestial smell ;—these are produced for ever.

Sutra (37) :—These are obstacles in (the way of) meditation; but perfections in the distractive (waking) state.

Com :—These—*i.e.* intuition and the rest appearing in one of meditative mind,—become obstacles; because they go against descriminative knowledge ; but appearing in those of distracted minds, these are so many perfections.

Sutra (38) :—From relaxation of the cause of bondage, and by a knowledge of the method of passing, (proceeds) the entrance of the mind into another body.

Com :—Of the fickle and unsteady mind, the confinement in the body is due to the force of karmic residua. The relaxation of this karma which is the cause of bondage is brought about by the force of meditation. The knowledge of the method of passing of the mind too is produced by meditation. On the decay of karma, and by the knowledge of the process of his own mind, the yogi infuses his mind into other bodies, after extracting it from his own. The mind thus infused becomes correlated to the senses; just as the bees follow their chief both when flying out and flying in, so the mind entering into another body is followed by the senses.

Sutra (39) :—**From the subdual of *udána*, ascension and non-contact with water, mud, thorns and the like.**

Com :—The function of the aggregate of the senses, characterised by Prâṇa and the rest, constitutes Life. Its action is fivefold : (1) The *Prâna*, extending from the heart and proceeding by the mouth and the nostrils ; (2) the *Samâna*, extending to the navel, so called from its levelling tendency; (3) the *Apâna*, extending to the soles of the foot, so called from its declining or descending tendency; (4) the *Udâna*, extending to the head, so called from its ascending tendency ; (5) the pervading *Vyâna*. Of these *Prâna* is the chief. From mastery over *Udâna* results non-contact with water, mud, thorns, &c, as also ascension at the time of death. The operator attains to it in the character of Vaśî (master).

Sutra (40) :—**From mastery over *Samána*, effulgence.**

Com :—One who has subdued the Samána burns (after death), by the fire raised out of his own body.

Sutra (41) :—**From Sanyama over the relation between the organ of hearing and âkâsa, perfect audition.**

Com :—All auditory organs as also all sound have their abidance in Âkása; as has been declared : "Those who have their audition extending over equal areas, have it limited to one area" (*Panchasikha*). (*i.e.* all organ of hearing exist in Akása). This is the charactcristic of Akása, as also is *unveiledness.* Similarly, there being no covering for the unbodied, Akâsa comes to have the property of omnipresenee. The organ of hearing is inferred from the perception of sound of two persons, deaf and otherwise : one perceives the sound, and the other does not. Therefore it is only the organ of hearing which has sound for its object. To one who has practised Sanyama over the relation of the organ of hearing and Âkâsa, accrues perfect audition.

Sutra (42) :—From the Sanyama over the relation of the body and Âkâsâ, (results) passage through space, from the acquisition of levity like that of cotton.

Com :—Wherever there is body, there is also Ââksa, because it is this latter that gives it room. The relation between these is that of approach; from having Sanyama over this and thereby subduing the relation, and acquiring the levity of light objects like cotton down to the atom, and thereby subduing the aforesaid relation, the yogi becomes buoyant ; and by this buoyancy the yogi is able to walk on the surface of water; and also supporting himself by the spider's thread, he wanders in the luminous rays of the Sun; and thence proceeds his unobstructed passage in space.

Sutra (43):—The external, unthought of junction (of the mind) is the "Great Incorporeal"; thence the falling off of the veil of illumination.

Com :—The junction of the mind outside the body is called the "incorporeal" Dhâraṇâ. It is called "kalpitá (thought of) when it is only the external function of the mind abiding in the body. When on the other hand, it is the external function of the mind outside the body, and as such independent of it,—then it is called the "*Akalpita*" (unthought of). Out of these two the yogi by the "thought," accomplishes the "unthought" Great Incorporeal, by means of which he enters other bodies. From this *Dhâranâ* results the falling of the veil—the threefold function of afflictions and karma, originating in foulness and darkness—of the Buddhic goodness which has the nature of illumination.

Sutra (44):—Mastery over the elements, from the *Sanyama* with reference to grossness, character, subtlety, concomitance and usefulness.

Com :—The specific qualities sound and the rest, belonging to the Earth &c., together with the properties of *shape* and the rest, are named "gross;" this is the first form of the elements. The second form is their respective generic characteristic :—E. G. shape for the Earth, viscidity for the Water, heat for Fire, velocity for Air, omnipresence for Âkâsa,—all this is what is included in the term "character." The specific forms of these generic ones, are Sound and the rest. As has been declared: "Of these (elements) included in one class (that of "Element"), the only" differentiation is through their distinguishing properties." In this system, Substance is the aggregate of the generic and specific characteristics. Because the aggregate exists in a two-fold manner—(1) One in which the distinct names of the constituent members are suppressed—as 'body,' 'tree' 'forest,' 'crowd' &c ; and (2) that in which the constituent members are mentioned—as 'both men and gods',—of which one portion are the 'men' and the other the 'gods ;' and it is only by means of these two portions, that it is called an "aggregate." Again the aggregate may be through difference as well as non-difference, (1) as 'the grove of mangoes', 'a crowd of Brahmanas' (the genitive case always implying difference); (2) as "mango-grove' 'Brahmana-crowd' (there being non-difference of the aggregate from its constituent members). This again is two-fold : (1) Those that have their constituent members separated from another, and (2) those whose constituent members are not so separated. As examples of the first we have 'forest' 'crowd' &c (where the members forming the crowd exist separately); and as those of (2) we have, 'tree', 'body' and the like (which, have these members consisting in themselves). Of these, Substance belongs to this second kind of aggregates—so holds Patanjali. Thus has been explained the "form."

Now what is the subtile form of these? (Reply :) The Rudimentary Elements, from which the gross Elements take their rise. The only constituent member of these is the atom, consisting of the generic and specific (characteristics); and thus these form an aggregate of the class of those having their constituent members coexisting. The same case holds with all rudimentary elements. This is the third, "Subtlety."

Now begins (the consideration of) the fourth form of the elements : The attributes being of the nature of illumination, activity and inertness correlated to the character of their respective effects,—are mentioned by the word "concomitance."

Their fifth form is "usefulness", *fruition*; the character of being for the purpose of experience and emancipation belonging to the attributes, and the attributes being related to the elements, gross as well rudimentary, as also to the elemental objects (jar, cow &c.),—all come to have a purpose.

Thus then from Sanyama over the above-mentioned five forms, results the perception as well as the subdual of these. Of these, by subduing the five elemental forms, the yogi becomes the "conqueror of the elements"; and therefrom the elements along with Nature follow the dictates of his will—just as the cow follows its calf.

Sutra (45):—Therefrom proceed Attenuation and the rest; as also perfection of the body, and the non-destruction of its functions.

Com:—Of these, Attenuation is that whereby the Yogi becomes atomic; Levity or Buoyancy is that whereby he becomes light; by Illimitability he becomes great; by *Prápti*(Approach)he touches the moon by the finger-tip; "Irresistible Will" is the non-frustration of desires,whereby he sinks in and rises to the surface of the earth as in water; by "Subjection" he becomes the subduer of the elements and other objects, being himself unsubdued by others; by "Supremacy" he becomes the dispenser of the origin, dissolution and position of the elements; "Fulfilment of Desires" is the truthfulness of one's determination—*i.e.*, the disposition of the elements and their causes in accordance with his will or determination. Though having the power, he does not change the nature of things (does not make a moon of the sun and so on). Why? Because of their having been determined by the will of the Primeval Perfect Being (God) of the irresistible will. These are the eight Perfections or Occult Powers.

"The perfection of the body" will be explained in the next aphorism.

"The non-obstruction of its functions"—the earth does not obstruct, by its shape, the actions of the yogi's body, in as much as he enters even the stone; the viscid water wets him not; nor does the hot fire burn him; nor does the fast wind move him; and lastly even in the unveiled Akasa, he has his body veiled, in as much as he is invisible even to the Perfect Ones.

Sutra (46) :—**Beauty (symmetry of form), Loveliness, Strength, and Adamantine Toughness (of the body) constitute Bodily Perfection.**

Com :—(The Yogi is) beautiful, lovely bright, with superb strength, and with an adamantine body.

Sutra (47) :—**From Sanyama with regard to perception, nature, egoism, concomitance and usefulness, results mastery over the sense-organs.**

Com :—Sound and the rest in their generic and the specific forms, constitute the *perceived* ; the function of the senses with regard to this is *perception*; and this does not consist in the perception of the generic form alone ; for how could the mind perceive any object together with its specific forms which has not been perceived ?

"Nature"—substance—sense-organ—is the aggregate "with coexisting constituents," of the specific and generic (effects) of the Buddhic Sattva which is of the nature of illumination.

Their third form is self-consciousness consisting in "egoism" —the generic form of which the senses are the specific forms.

The fourth form are the Attributes, of the nature of Illumination, Activity and Inertness, consisting in ascertainment (the property of Buddhi,) which is constituted by the three attributes ;—whereof the sense-organs together with self-consciousness, are the modifications.

The fifth form is the character of the Attributes,—that of being for the soul's purpose.

From gradually performing Sanyama over these five forms, the yogi subdues each of them separately—and from this fivefold conquest proceeds the mastery ever the senses.

Sutra (48) :—Therefrom (proceed) fleetness like that of mind, un-instrumental perception, and complete mastery over Nature.

Com :—The acquiring of the supernatural movement of the body is "Fleetness like that of mind."

"Uninstrumental perception" is the functioning of the senses of the Incorporeal (yogi) in accordance with the time, place and object desired by him.

"Mastery over Nature" is supremacy over all the modifications of Nature.

These three perfections are called "Honey-like," and proceed from the aforesaid mastery over the five sense-organs.

Sutra (49) :—Just as one has distinctive knowledge of the attribute of *Sattva* and Spirit, (their results) supremacy over all conditions, and also omniscience.

Com :—To one who rejoices in the supreme effulgence (the High Vashîkara) of Buddhic goodness freed from all taint of Foulness and Darkness ;—and who thus abides solely in the distinctive knowledge of Goodness and Spirit,—to such a one accrues the "supremacy over all conditions"—*i. e.*, all kinds of attributes, active and passive, repair to the absolute vision of their Lord, the Knower of the Field—(Spirit). "Omniscience"—the simultaneous discriminative knowledge of the universal attributes, existing in their past, present and future states. This is the Vishoka (Sorrowless) Perfection, by attaining to which, the yogi becoming omniscient, wanders about, on the falling off of the bondage of distractions (or afflictions).

Sutra (50):—From indifference even thereto, follows Isolation, the seed of evils having been destroyed.

Com :—When on the decay of trouble and actions, the yogi cogitates thus—" this distinctive cognition is a property of goodness which is among the avoidables, and the Soul is unmodifying and pure, other than Goodness "—then of this disattached yogi, the seeds of trouble becoming unproductive, like the burnt paddy-seed, disappear together with the mind. And those having disappeared, the Soul does not again experience the three-fold pain. Thus the isolation of the Soul consists in his absolute separation from the attributes whose purpose has been fulfilled, and who are manifested in the form of the function of karmic troubles; then alone results the soul's abidance in his own pure—*i.e.* pure Sentience.

Sutra (51):—(There should be) avoidance of association with, and pride in, celestial temptations, for there is possibility of reccurrence of evils.

Com :—There are four kinds of yogis :—(1) Prathamakalpika (neophyte of the first stage), (2) the Madhupratika, (3) The Prajnâjyoti, and (4) The Atikrântabhavaniya: Of these, the one whose light (of intuition) has begun to operate is the first. The second is the " truth-supporting-wisdom. " The subduer of the elements and the sense-organs is the third,—one who has taken protective measures towards that which has been felt (the conquest of the senses), and equipped with the means for the accomplishment of that which is to be felt (the vishoka &c.). The fourth is one who has gone beyond feeling ; the one purpose of such a one is the retrograde activity (dissolution) of the mind ; and to him belongs the sevenfold knowledge of the last stage.

17

To the Brahmana directly perceiving the Madhumati stage, the gods—perceiving the purity of his goodness—invite him to the powers: "Well! come and enjoy yourselves here! Desirable are these pleasures! And desirable is this girl! This drug stops old age and death! Airy is this conveyance! These are the Kalpa-trees! Sacred is the celestial Ganga! Perfect are the great Rishis! Excellent and agreeable are the Apsaras! Supernatural the Eye and the Ear! Adamantine the body! Thou hast acquired a right to all this by thy qualities,—so come and have recourse to this undying undecaying abode, loved of the Gods."

Being thus invited, the yogi is to think over the faults of attachment in this manner: "Being broiled in the fire of metempsychosis, and passing through the dark abyss of birth and death, I have somehow or other acquired this light of yoga, the dispeller of the darkness of troubles. Of this light the airy objects (of sense) born of desire, are the opponents. So how am I, having acquired this light, to be deceived by a miragic longing for the sensuous objects, and thus make to burn in myself the dying embers of the fires of metempychosis? So good bye, to you all dreamy sensuous objects, the desired of poor people!" In this determined attitude the yogi is to sit for meditation. Having avoided association, he is also to avoid pride—*i. e.*, (he is not to take pride) in the fact of his being invited even by the gods, because steeped in this pride and considering himself safe, he will not perceive himself caught up by the hair by Death. And then will negligence,—looking for another hole (discrepancy) in his conduct, and only suppressible by constant watchfulness, finding the above loophole,—will enliven the (sleeping) afflictions. Thence the possibility of evils. Thus for one who avoids both association and pride, the contemplated end will be strengthened, and the end to be contemplated will come up to the front.

Sutra (52):—From Sanyama over the moments and their order, the knowledge born of discrimination.

Com:—As the smallest division of matter is the atom, so the smallest division of time is the *moment*–which is the time taken by the motion of an atom from one place to another ; and the uninterrupted flow of this is "order." Of moment and its order there is no aggregate ; therefore Day, Month &c. are only aggregates of so many cognitions (each coming in one moment). Thus Time is devoid of reality, being a mere creation of the mind; but being correlated to the verbal cognitions, it appears as a distinct entity to ordinary people in the distracted state. The Moment thus becoming objective (*i. e.*, an entity in itself) becomes also related to the (assumed) order ; this order consists in the non-interruption of two moments,—to this (order) the time-knowing yogis give the name 'Time.' Two moments cannot occur together ; for no order is possible for any two things occurring simultaneously. Order is the sequence of the following moment from the preceding one. Therefore the present is the only moment, there being none either past or future ; and as such there is no collective term for it (as *Time*). The future and the past moments (those that are popularly so called) are to be explained as referring to the different modifications. Thus by means of a single moment does all the world experience modifications ; and all the properties are mere encumbrances on this single moment.

By the Sanyama over this moment and its order, there is direct perception of these, and thence proceeds the knowledge born of discrimination.

The particular object of the knowledge is now described :

Sutra (53):—Therefrom results the knowledge of the (difference of) two similars, when that dif-

ference is not marked out by kind, character or position.

Com:—Two similar objects ressembling each other in position and character, the ground of difference exists in the difference of kind,—as in the case of the *cow* and the *horse*. When there is similarity of position and kind, then it exists in that of character—as the Kalakshi cow, and the Swastimati cow Of two fruits of the same kind and character, the ground of difference lies in the difference of their position—one above and the other below (in a tree). If however at the time of coming across the first, the mind of the agent is absorbed in the other, and as such the first one also is brought over to the place of the second, then the order of position becomes inexplicable by the ordinary process; but it comes from discriminative knowledge free from all doubt. How? The place occupied by the first fruit is different from that occupied by the second fruit; and these two fruits differ by the recognition of their respective positions; and the ground of difference between these two is the recognition of their respective positions. By this example it is shown that the Yogi recognises the difference between two atoms similar in kind, character and position, by the direct perception of the time and place related to the first atom, the perception of the place of the second atom being due to impossibility of the former place being occupied by the second atom simultaneously with the first.

Others on the other hand describe the process thus:—"It is the final specific property that produces the knowledge of difference. But in this case also the ground of difference is the difference in position and character, as also the difference in shape and kind. The difference in time is amenable to the perception of the yogi only." Hence it has been declared:

"There is no real difference, in the absence of the differences of shape and kind" says *Vârshagaṇya*.

Sutra (54):—The knowledge born of discrimination is emancipative, omni-objective, semper-objective and simultaneous.

Com:—"*Emancipative*"—Intuitional or non-experiential (*vide* III. 33) "*Omniobjective*"—there is nothing that is not perceptible to it.

"*Semper-objective*"—knowing everything in all forms and conditions and at all times, past, present and future.

"*Simultaneous*"—perceiving every thing in every way, at the same moment.

Such is the knowledge born of discrimination, in its complete form. The light of yoga is a part hereof, so long as it is accomplished by resting on the "honeyed" stage.

To one who has acquired discriminative knowledge or to one who has not there accrues.

Sutra (55):—Islation on the equality of the purity of Goodness and Soul.

Com:—When Buddhic Goodness being washed clear of all taint of Foulness and Darkness, and having its activity restricted to the recognition of the difference of goodness and the soul, the seed of troubles is burnt up, and then the Buddhi becomes similar to the Soul in purity. The purity of the Soul consists in the absence of all imposed experience. Under such circumstances, results Isolation to the perfect as well as to the imperfect,—to one who has discriminative knowledge, and to one who has not. On the attainment of wisdom by one who has burnt up the seeds of trouble there is no need for anything. Perfections born of meditation as well as wisdom, are all included in the said Sattwic purity. As a matter of fact however wisdom dispels the want of perception or ignorance, on the suppression whereof the resultant troubles cease to come forth; and the absence of the troubles leads to absence of karmic fruition. In this state, the attributes, having all their functions finished, do not present themselves again to the soul's sight,—and in this lies the Soul's Isolation. In this state the Soul becomes isolated, shines in the pure effulgence of his own pristine form.

Section IV.

OF ISOLATION.

Sutra (1) :—The occult powers are produced by birth, herbs, incantations, austerities, or Meditation.

Com :—The Power due to birth is brought about by corporeal change. "*By herbs:*" *e. g.*, the medicinal preparations in the house of the Asuras (*i e.*, *Pâtâla*). "*By incantations.*" Such as the acquirement of "Molecularity" (*Aṇimâ*), the capability of approaching the sky. "*By austerities*" the accomplishment of desire, *e. g.*, being capable of attaining to any desirable form, the yogi moves about here, there and everywhere, in accordance with his own unimpeded will. The Powers due to Meditation have already been described.

Notes :—(1) "*Corporeal change*"—Sometimes the actions of the yogi in his earthly life are developed to such an extent that he is directly born among the gods, with a celestial body, and as such molecularity and the rest come to him naturally.

(2) "*Have been described*"—in the foregoing section.

Of the body and the sense-organs, developed into another kind,—

Sutra (2) :—The transformation into another kind (results) from the transmutation of the material cause.

Com :—The previous form having been disolved, the production of the following change is due to a re-arrangement of the constituent particles. The material causes of the body and the sense-organs, in helping their modifications or effects, by means of transmutation, depend upon such instrumental causes as virtue and the rest.

Notes :—"*Transmutation of the material cause*"—The material cause of the body are the five elements Earth and the rest, and that of the sense-organs is Self-consciousness; and the 'transmutation' mentioned in the aphorism consists in there-arrangement of the various particles making up such causes. It is this transmutation, brought about by the past actions (virtuous or otherwise, of the agent), which leads to the change of the kind of body and the sense-organs. *e.g.*, various deeds tend to transmute the particles of the elements &c., in such a manner as to bring about a celestial body for the agent.

Sutra (3):—To the material causes, the instrument is non-efficient; from it (proceeds) the piercing of the covering,—as in the case of the husbandman.

Com:—The instruments in the shape of virtue &c., are no helps to the mutations of the material causes; for certainly the cause is not urged by the effect. How then? "*From it proceeds the piercing of the covering &c.*," As the husbandman,—desiring to irrigate, from a full supply of water in one field, another field in the same plane, or in one lower or higher,—does not carry the water by means of his hands, but only cuts through the bunds, on the opening of which the water of itself flows through the adjoining field;—so in the same manner, virtue pierces the covering of the material causes, in the shape of vice, on the removal whereof, the material causes of their own accord, supply their various modifications. Or again, as the same husbandman in the same field is not capable of supplying either liquid or solid ingredients to the root of the paddy; what he does is to remove from the field all foreign weeds and plants, on the removal whereof the ingredients of themselves enter into the paddy-roots; so in the same manner, virtue is only the cause of the suppression of vice—purity and impurity being diametrically opposed to each other—and it is no cause in the operation of the material cause. In this connection Nandiswara and others, should be quoted as examples. On the other hand vice also only tends to suppress virtue; and then follows the change into impurity—*e.g.* Nahusha changed into an Ajagara serpent and the like.

When the yogi creates (for himself) many bodies, then, have all of these one and the same mind, or has each of these a separate mind? Reply:

Sutra (4):—The created internal organs proceed from Self-consciousness alone.

Com:—The yogi produces the created internal organ with the help only of Self-consciousness, the cause of internal organs. Consequently each body has a (separate) internal organ.

Sutra (5):—In the diverse tendency of the many, the impelling internal organ is one.

Com:—"How should the action of many internal organs follow the tendency of the one internal organ?"—(thinking thus, the yogi) makes one internal organ such as urges the others to action. Thence follows the diversity of action.

Notes:—(1) "In the preceding aphorism, the question having been solved as to how a single individual can provide thinking principles for many bodies, the question arises as to how can many thinking principles act in concert and preserve the unity of the creator? If this unity be not admitted, there would be so many independent individuals, each following the bent of his own mind; and the idea of one individual acting as many without any loss of individuality would be lost. This doubt is removed by the explanation that the thinking principles provided to the many are in reality one, and entirely controlled by the primary thinking principle (that which is related to the occult power displayed), of which they are mere scintillations"—Rajendra Lal Mitra—"*Yogasutras*"

Sutra (6):—Thereof the contemplation-born is without impressions or residua.

Com:—The created internal organs are of five kinds, the occult powers being due to (1) birth, (2) herbs, (3) incantations, (4) austerities and (5) meditation. Of these, the internal organ which is brought about by contemplation, is without residua,—that is to say, it is free from all tendency to attachment and the like ; and for this reason it has no connection with virtue and vice ; because the yogi has had all his troubles ended ; for others (besides the yogi), there is an accumulation of karmic impressions.

Notes :—(1) "*And for this reason &c.*"—The connection of virtue and vice being due to attachment &c.

Sutra (7):—The actions of the Yogi are neither white nor black; those of others are of three kinds.

Com :—The classes of actions are fourfold—(1) the black, (2) the white-black, (3) the white,—and (4) the non-white-non-black. Of these the black kind belongs to the evil-minded. The white-black, is performable by external means ; and in connection with this, the accumulation of karmic residua is due to the infliction of pain and doing of kindness to others ; the white one belongs to those given to penance, study and contemplation ; this kind, being confined solely to the internal organ, cannot be performed by external means, and as such, is not due to the infliction of pain on others. The "Non-white-non-black" belongs to the Sanyasis, whose troubles are at an end and who are equipped with the final or highest body only. Of these, to the Yogi belongs the non-white because he has renounced all desire for fruition—, and the non-white—because of non-acceptance. Those of other beings, are of the former three kinds.

Notes :—(1) "*The Black*" &c.,—The 'black' being due to Darkness leads to pain such as animal slaughter ; the 'white-black' being due to Foulness leads to pleasure ending in pain, as the offering of sacrifices and the like ; the 'white' due to pure Goodness leads to

unalloyed pleasure, such as study, contemplation and the like; the fourth is beyond the reach of the attributes, and as such free from both pleasure and pain.

(3) "*Because he has renounced &c*"—He is untouched by the effects of virtuous deeds because he has renounced all desire for their effects in the shape of future aggrandisement; and he is free also from the effects of the vicious actions because such he never performs.

(3) "*Infliction of pain and doing of kindness &c.*"—As for instance in a sacrifice, much pain is inflicted on the animals that take part therein; and kindness is shown when the priests are handsomely paid for their services.

Sutra (8):—Thence is the manifestation of the impressions or residua which are suitable to its fruition.

Com:—"*Thence*" *i.e.*,from the threefold action "*which are suitable to its fruition*"—*i.e*, suitable to the particular fruition of actions of particular kinds; that is to say, those residua that help the fruition of the action,—of these alone there is the manifestation. For a celestial or godly action, in its function, can never lead to the manifestation of the infernal, the brutal or the human residua; on the contrary, what is manifested or enlivened (thereby) is only the residua that are conformable to celestial existence. The same consideration holds respecting the hellish, the bestial and the human (actions).

Notes:—(1) *Of particular kinds*"—*i.e.*, actions either virtuous or otherwise.

Sutra (9):—On account of the uniformity of memory and impressions (*residua*), there is sequence or *uninterruptibility of relation*, even after breaks by class, locality and time.

Com:—The beginning of the fruition of the action leading to the feline birth, is always enlivened or manifested by the particular manifesting cause which leads to its manifestation;

and as such, if this fruition,—even though removed or interrupted either by hundreds of species or by great distance, or by hundreds of cycles,—again happens to become manifested only through its own special manifested causes; then it becomes vivid by taking hold of the residua brought about by the previous experience of feline birth. Why? Because, of these (residua), the only manifesting cause is an analogous action, even though they may be removed therefrom; and in this manner there is an uninterruptibility or continuity of relation (between the residua and its analogous manifesting action). Why? Because "of the uniformity of memory and the impressions". (That is to say)—As the experiences, so the impressions; and these latter are exactly similar to the Karmic residua; and lastly as the residua, so the memory (or Instinct). Thus we see that memory or instinct is due to impressions removed therefrom by class, locality and time. This memory again produces impressions. Thus these impressions due to memory are manifested by the force of the attainment of the function of Karmic residua. Consequently, even of the interrupted (actions and fruition) the sequence is established, on account of the uninterruptibility of the causal relation.

Notes:—(1) "*These are exactly similar to the Karmic residua*"—The purport is that, as the *apurva*, the Unseen Force, though produced by transitory actions, is yet lasting and capable of bringing about its effects after a time; so in the same manner impressions, though produced by fleeting experiences, are yet lasting.

(2) "*attainment of the function &c.*"—i.e., by the rousing or vivifying energy of the karmic residua.

(3) "According to the preceding aphorism, the residua of the former births are the causes of manifestation of certain effects; but since concomitance is necessary between cause and effect, while the intervention of many dissimilar births between two similar causes an interruption, it may be urged that residua are not the cause of memory, as alleged. The objection is met by saying that the memory remains, and therefore the sequence is, obviously, not broken"

Mitra.

Sutra (10) —Besides there is no beginning about them, because of the eternity of desire.

Com :—Of these residua there is no beginning, because of the eternity of desire. The selfish desire—"may I not cease to exist," "may I live"—met with in every individual, cannot be said to be natural (product, and as such not eternal). Why? (Because), How else, would there be,—for the newly born infant who has not yet experienced death—any fear of death, which is due only to aversion and pain? For certainly a natural object does not admit of a cause (instrumental cause). The fact therefore is, that the internal organ chained to eternal residua, through certain causes, gets hold of some of the residua, and then comes forward for the experience of the spirit.

Other theorists have asserted that the internal organ is expansive and contractible, like the jar-and-mansion lamp; and as such, it is of the same form as that of the body; and thus would be explained its existence in this interrim, as also its rebirth. The Masters however lay down that, what is expansive and contractible is only the function of the internal organ, which of itself is omnipresent. This (internal organ) again is dependent on causes such as virtue and the like. The cause again is of two kinds—external and internal; the former is such as is due to bodily means—e. g., hymn-singing, charity and reverence; the latter depending on the internal organ alone,—e. g., faith and the like. As is declared: "The pastimes of the Yogi, friendship and the like, are naturally independent of external means, and (as such) bring about the highest virtue" Of these two causes, the mental is the stronger. Why? Because, what can supersede wisdom and dispassion? who can render the Dandaka forest bare by bodily action, without mental strength? and who can drink up the ocean, like Agastya?

Notes :—(1) "*How else...aversion and pain*" : Supply here: 'if you do not accept the residua of pain caused by death, which occurred in the previous births'—This objection is levelled against the atheists who assert that everything is the product of nature, and deny the existence of anything eternal.

(2) "*For certainly a natural object &c.*"—anything that is due to mere nature cannot be dependent on any cause, like the heat of fire.

(3) "*The internal organ through certain causes &c.*"—Such a cause is the action whose time of function happens to arrive at the time being.

(4) "*Gets hold of &c.*"—i. e., such residua become manifested.

(5) "*Like the jar—&—mansion lamp*"—The light of a lamp is contracted or expands, according as it happens to be placed in a jar or in a large house; similarly the internal organ, through its substrate being either that of a feline or an elephantine body, would contract or expand, and as such would be small or large accordingly; and such the mind can be said to be of the same size as the body it happens to occupy. This theory is opposed to the atomic character of the mind, as laid down by Kanada and his followers. The view of the author himself is that the mind is neither atomic, nor dependent on the size of its substrate; but it is vast, or omnipresent.

(6) "*Its presence &c.*"—During cyclic dissolution the mind is said to be living in the subtle body, and hence of the same form ; and it is this subtle body equipped with the aforesaid mind which takes its birth again in the following cycle. Thus according to these theorists, such existence of the internal organ between two births can only be explained by making the mind depend for its form on the body it occupies ; according to the author however the mind is ominpresent, and as such there is no difficulty in explaining any facts with regard to it.

(7) "*The highest virtue*"—i. e., the white action (see above).

Sutra (11).—Being held together by cause, effect, substratum and support, the absence of these would produce their absence.

Com :—"*Cause*"—From virtue results pleasure, and from vice pain ; from pleasure proceeds attachment and from pain aversion ; thence follows endeavour ; and the agent acting through this endeavour, by mind, words and body, tends to favour one individual and hurt the other ; thence follow virtue and vice, pleasure and pain, attachment and aversion, —this operation constitutes the wheel of metempsychosis; of this ever-turning wheel, the guiding force is Ignorance; the root of all troubles. Such is the "cause."

"*The effect*" is that on which is based the existence of virtue and the rest; (for) there is no production of that which never before existed. The mind, equipped with its faculties, is the "substratum" of the residua; as when the faculties of the mind have been destroyed, the residum cannot continue to exist, for want of a substratum.

That with a view to which an object enlivens a particular residuum, is the "support" of such a residuum.

Thus, all residua, being held together by these—cause, effect, substratum and support—, when these latter cease to exist, there follows the absence of the residua based upon them.

Notes:—(1) The aphorism answers the question—how can the eternal be undone? The purport of the reply is that, since desires are the sum total of cause, effect, substratum and support, one has to remove those conditions which produce desires, and that removal *ipso facto* removes desires.

(2) "*There is no production &c.*"—This is added in order to meet the following objection: "How can there be any permanent conglomeration of the cause with the effect? Or again, how can the absence of the effect lead to the absence of the cause? For certainly the cause exists even during the absence of the effect." The sense of the reply is that, we deny the production of any entity that never existed (see *Sankhyakarika*—9). All that we attribute to the present cause is the faculty of manifesting the effect which has all along lain latent in its material cause. And of course the permanent conglomeration of the cause with the effect becomes quite compatible when considered with reference to the effect in its latent state.

(Objection):—'There is no production for a non-entity; nor is there any destruction of an entity; under the circumstances, how would the residua, being entities, be undone?"—(Reply)—

Sutra (12) :—**Past and Future exist in real nature, in consequence of the difference in the conditions of the properties.**

Com :—That which *is to be* is the "*future*", and that which *has been* is the "*past*", and that which *is fulfilling its function* is the *present*. These three are cognisable by (Yogic) cognition. If these did not exist in reality, then there would be no cognition, without an object. Therefore the past and the future do exist in reality. And further, if the agency bringing about the effects of actions— partaking either of enjoyment or of Isolation—were a nonentity, then the endeavour of experts with a view to—*i.e.*, by means of—that (agency) would be inexplicable. The cause is capable only of exhibiting to the present time the already existing effect (lying latent), and not of bringing forth an altogether new entity. A perfectly established cause only helps the effect in a particular way, but does not produce any thing new.

An object is always endowed with a number of properties; and such properties exist in accordance with different conditions. And though the present, being related to a certain individual, exists materially, yet the same cannot be said with regard to the *past* and the *future*. How then? The *future* exists in its *manifestible* (that which *is to be* manifested) form; as the *past* exists in the individual that *has been*. The *manifestation* of form is only possible for the *conditions* of the *present*; and it is not possible for those of the *past* or of the *future*. And during the existence of our condition, it is quite compatible that the other two conditions should exist in close relationship with the (same) object; hence the existence of the three conditions is not preceded by their non-existence.

Sutra (13) :—They are individualised (manifested) or subtile and consist in attributes.

Com :—The aforesaid properties, having the three conditions, consist in the individualised—*i. e.*, in the present—and in the subtile—*i. e.*, the past and future, these latter forming the six *non-specific* elements. All these however are only particular formations of the Attributes, and hence, in reality, are of the nature of these Attributes. As says the authoritative injunction : "The highest form of the Attributes does not come within the range of vision ; what does come within visual range is altogether insignificant, like (Mâyâ)."

Notes : (1)—"The simple proposition in this aphorism is that all properties are mere modifications of the three primary Attributes (Goodness, Foulness, and Darkness) circumstances may make them subtile or gross ; but, whether one or the other, they consist of nothing but the three Attributes...modified in some form or another. They are mere modes of being, but not radically different beings."—*Mitra.*

(2) "*The six non-specific &c.*"—The *Yogavartika* does not admit of this reading

(3) "*Injunction*"—This quotation is said to be from a work on Sankhya by the Rishi Varshaganya, named in the *Sankhya Tattwa—Kaumudi.*

If all objects on the Attributes, how do you explain (the singular use, such as) "*one* word," "one sense"? Reply :

Sutra (14) :—From unity of modification (results) the one-ness of a thing.

Com :—Of the Attributes,—capable of illumination, activity and inertness—and of the nature of the means of perception (*grahana*),—there is one modification though the form of a sense—organ, constituting the ear, a sense-orgain and of (the same attributes) being of the nature of the object of perception there is another modification through the form of sound, making sound the object; of sound and the rest, ressembling each other in form, there is one modification, the earth-atom, having for its components the rudimentary elements; and of these (sound &c.) again, there is another modification the earth,—the cow, the tree, the mountain and the like; similarly among the other elements, there can be only a single common modification, based on their respective properties, viscidity, heat, elasticity (*pranamitwa*) and spaciousness (*avakasadána*).

" There is no object which is not accompained by an idea; on the other hand, we have ideas not accompained by any object such as those occuring in a dream "—The Nihilists who in this manner set aside the reality of the form of the object asserting, as they do, that 'the object is only the creation of an idea, like objects of a dream, and it does not exist in reality';—how can these persons be believed who despise and abandon the reality of the object, on the strength of the untruthful knowledge of vikalpa,...the object which has by means of its inherent capability presented itself before him in its real form?

Wherefore is this improper—? Reply:

Sutra (15):—Notwithstanding the sameness of the object, the course of the two are distinct, from diversity of the internal organ.

Com:—A single object, occupying many internal organs, is (said to be) 'common'; and this (object) is not due to the agency of a single internal organ (or mind), nor to that of many minds; it exists by itself. How? Because of the diversity of minds, notwithstanding the sameness of the object. That is to say, even on the sameness of the object, the mind has the idea of pleasure, through virtue, and also the idea of pain from the same object, through vice ; from the same the idea of delusion, through ignorance ; and lastly from that very object, the idea of indifference through right vision. Under such circumstances, to whose mind can such an object owe its existence ? Certainly it is not likely that the object created by one mind should affect another mind. Consequently of the *object* and the *idea* (or cognition),—distinct from each other on account of their respective characters of the cognisable and the cogniser.—the course is distinct ; and there is not the slightest tinge of any confusion among these.

According to the Sankhya view again, the object is endowed with the three Attributes ; and the function of the Attributes is mobile ; hence the object is related to the minds through the instrumentality of virtue and the rest, and through its different forms, becomes the cause of the different cognitions, appearing in accordance with the aforesaid instruments.

Notes : (1) A simple object gives rise to different ideas in different minds, through the difference in the action of the three Attributes (*Vide Sankhya-tattva-kaumudi*—, 7 and Bhoja's commentary.—" On beholding an attractive woman, pleasure is felt by an amorous person, pain by her rival, and disgust by an ascetic.

(2) " *and certainly it is not likely &c.*"—For if it were so, the one person's cognition of redness would produce the same idea in the minds of all persons.

Some people have thus declared : "The object is coexistent with cognition, because it is cognisable, like pleasure and the like "—These people by this means set aside the commonality (of object and cognition, mentioned above), and thus deprive the object by of its character, at all times, past as well as present.

(To these subjective Idealists it is replied.)—

Sutra (16) :—Nor is the object dependent upon a single mind ;—(because) what would it be when not cognised by that ?

Com :—If the object depended upon a single mind, then, if that mind were either confounded or suppressed, then the form of the object would not be apprehended thereby ; nor would it be amenable to any other mind (being dependent upon the former alone) ; and as such it would become "uncognised" (apramáṇaka) ; *i.e.*, its character would not be comprehended by any one ; under such circumstances, what would the object be ? Then again,being connected with the mind, whence would it be produced ? Those parts of the object which were not present (before the particular mind) would cease to be ; similarly the non-perception of the back (of a certain animal) would lead to the non-cognition of the stomach as well. For these reasons, the object must be independent, common to all perceiving agents. Minds too are independent and act differently with regard to each person. From the connection of these two (object and mind) results cognition (or perception), which constitutes the experience of the person.

Note : (1) This aphorism, which is left out by Bhoja, is meant to meet the following objection : "Granted, that the object is distinct from the cognition ; even then the object, being insentient, could not lead to the recognition of itself without cognition by which it is illuminated or manifested ; and as such the object can exist only along with cognition and not at any other time"—The difficulty is met by the aphorism by propounding the question—whence is the object produced ? If from the cognising agent, then is this agent, the cognising mind, one or many ? The latter alternative is impossible because opposed to general experience. If, however, the object were the result of a single mind, then on that particular mind ceasing to take notice of the object, the object would cease to exist ; and it would not be possible for any other person to notice it; which is opposed to all common experience.

Sutra (17) :—A thing is known or unknown, in consequence of the necessity of the mind being tinged by it.

Com :—The object, being of the natnre of a magnet, connects with itself and tinges the mind, which is of the nature of soft iron. The object whereby the mind is tinged, is *known* ; and all objects besides this are *unknown* ? Thus on account of the object being known and unknown, the mind is modifiable.

Notes :—(1) "*Being of the nature of a magnet &c.*"—Like the magnet, the object is devoid of all action in itself, but draws the iron-like active mind to itself by means of the sense-organs and tinges it—*i.e.*, moulds it into its own form.

(2) "*On account of the object being known &c.*"—*i. e.*, If the mind were not modifiable, the fact of the object being known or unknown would be inexplicable. This fact also serves to distinguish the mind from the spirit to whom all objects are *always* known.

He to whom such a mind itself is an object, to such a one—

Sutra 18:—The functions of the mind are always known, for its presiding spirit is unmodifiable.

Com:—If like the mind, the spirit also were liable to mutation then would its objects also, in the shape of the functions of the mind, be known and unknown, like sound and other objects. But the constant consciousness and perceptibility of the mind leads to the inference of the immutable (or constant) character of its presiding spirit.

The following question may arise—The mind itself may be illuminative of itself as well as of the objects, like fire ; against this it is declared—

Sutra (19):—It is not self-illuminative, since it is perceptible.

Com:—As the other senses,as well as sound and other objects, being perceptible, are not self-illuminative, so should also the mind be understood to be. Nor can fire be an instance here; because the fire does not illuminate its non-illuminated form. Moreover illumination is seen to follow the connection of the illuminated and the illuminator ; but such connection is not possible with regard to one's own form. And again, the assertion that "the mind is self-illuminating" literally means that it is not cognisable by any person.—*e. g.*, Space (Âkâsa) existing in it own nature, can never exist in any other object. But the actions of all living beings are seen to follow from the consciousness of the activities of their mind—*e. g.*, "I am angry," "I am afraid," "in this is my attachment, and to this my aversion,"—such consciousness would not be explicable, if the mind were not perceptible.

(1) "*Moreover illumination is seen to follow &c*"—All action is based on the relation of the actor, the action and the instrument; as cooking is based on the relation of the cook, the action of cooking and the article cooked; similarly illumination being an action, must also be based on a similar relation; but such relation is only possible among different objects and not in a single object.

(2) "*But the actions of all living beings &c*"—"This meets the theory of tho non-perceptibility of the mind (by the spirit).

Sutra (20) :—Two (objects) cannot be cognised at one and the same time.

Com:—At one and the same time, it is not possibe to cognise one's own form as well as that of others. The Nihilists hold that the *action, effect and cause* (*origin, action and instrument*) are all identical.

Note :—The meaning of the aphorism is that the mind cannot perform the two acts of perception and self-knowing at the same time, and therefore it is obvious that it cannot by itself be the cause of intelligence.

It may be held that the mind suppressed by its own nature is cognised by another mind, following close upon it.

(Reply)

***Sutra* (21) :—(If) cognition by another mind (be postulated),—there would be an infinity of cognitions and also an *admixture* (or *confusion*) of memory.**

Com : If the mind were perceived by another mind, then whereby would the cognition of that cognition be perceived? If by another cognition, and this last too by a fourth and so on, then we would be landed on a *regressus ad infinitum*,—and there would also arise a confusion of memory; for, so many as there are perceptions of cognitions to cognitions, as many would be the (corresponding) memories. And from this admixture would result the non-ascertainment (*i.e.*, uncertainty) of any one memory. Thus (we find that) the Nihilists have confounded everything, by denying spirit as the (one) cogniser of (all) cognitions. These Nihilists again assuming cogniser-ship at random, cease to be logical. Some of them assume a mere entity, and hold that there is a certain entity which discards the present five *skandhas* or 'bodies' and takes to other *skandhas*; and having asserted this much, they fight shy of the same (entity): Thus "for the sake of the dispassion of the form of great disgust for the *skandhas*, and for that of the non-production or suppression thereof, I will lead the continent life under a preceptor,"—having said this, they again turn to suppress the very existence of the entity. The Sankhya, Yoga and the other systems declare that the word "*swa*", denotes the lord of the mind, the spirit, the cogniser.

Notes: (1) "*Suppressed by its own nature*"—*i. e.*, on account of its destructibility.

(2) "Confusion or admixture of memory"—because on one idea being called to memory all its attendant ideas would arise to infinity; because the series of cognitions would be unbroken on account of all

of them being equally related to one another; and the memory of one cognition would hold with it the whole series; and it would be impossible to determine which is the particular idea that has been revived.

(3) "*Suppress the very existence of the entity*"—*i.e.*, by denying the spirit, they strike at the root of the denotation of the word "I." Here Vijnana Bhikshu: "These Nihilists by so doing become quite illogical, because on the one hand they deny the existence of the cogniser (the spirit), and on the other they accept and strive after spiritual beatitude &c."

How?

Sutra (22):—The non-transitional spirit (obtains) the consciousness of its own cognition, when it takes its form.

Com:—The sentient faculty, unmodifying and unchanging, being reflected in the *modifiable* (the mind), falls in with its functions; and the function of the cognition (or understanding) is said to be identical with that of the internal organ (mind), on accounts of its (the reflected sentient faculty) merely imitating the function of the mind which has attained the form of the superimposition of the sentient faculty. As is declared: "Neither the nether world, nor mountain caves nor darkness, nor the crevices of the ocean,—(none of these,) is the cave where the eternal Brahma is concealed; the wise call it the function of the mind, "pure and simple."

[Note:—The aphorism is capable of a double interpretation, the difference resulting from the construction of "*tadâkârâpattyâ.*" The clause may be taken to mean: (1) "When the soul *takes its form*" (*i. e.*) when the soul takes the form (of the mental function), and (2) "*When the mind takes the form* of the soul." At first sight the order of the *sutra* would favour the first interpretation, and Professor Dvivedi accepts this interpretation which is also noticed by Dr. Mitra as being based on the interpretation of some "later commentators." But a little consideration will show that the second interpretation is the proper one. Because as the Bhâshya says, when the soul is reflected in the mind, it is the reflecting object that should take the form of the reflected object, not otherwise. So it must be the mind that takes the form of the soul which is "unchanging" (*apratisankrama*), and as such cannot take the form of any other object. Vachaspati Misra favours this interpretation. He explains the aphorism thus: "The soul's consciousness of its own cognition (results) when the mind takes its form,—i. e., when the mind becomes the substratum of the reflection of the sentient faculty, and as such takes its form. As for example, even without any action of the moon, the clear rippling water reflecting the disc of the moon manifests the moon also as moving; in the same manner, even without any action of the sentient faculty, the mind reflecting the image of the sentient faculty manifests the sentient faculty as being active through its (the mind's) action, &c, and attaining to its character of the *experienced*, supplies the sentient faculty with the character of the *experiencer*."

The force of the argument here depends upon the distinction made between intelligence (sentient faculty) and the function of the understanding (cognition); for the soul, though intelligence itself, does not exercise any function.

It is for this reason that it is held (that)—

Sutra (23) :—The mind tinged by the seer and the seen, is (able to perceive) all objects.

Com :—The mind is tinged by the cognisable object, and being itself an object, is conjoined by the subjective (knowing) soul to its functions; thus does the mind become 'tinged by the seer and the seen';— *i. e.*, enlivened by the object and the subject, and fallen in with the forms of the sentient and the insentient,-and appearing non-objective though really objective, and sentient though really insentient,—'resembling the rockcrystal,'—is said (to be able to perceive) all objects. It is for this reason that certain people being led away by this similarity of the mind, have declared it as alone sentient. Others again hold that all this is mere mind; any other object, cow or pot &c. together with its cause does not exist. All these (theorists) deserve to be pitied. Why? Because for their mistake, there is a ground in the shape of the mind enlivened by every kind of form. Consequently in meditative consciousness the object cognised being a reflection, is distinct from it (the mind), because of its (the mind) being its substratum. If this object were only the mind, then how would the form of conciousness be ascertained by consciousness itself? For these reasons, it is the Spirit by whom is determined or ascertained, in consciousness, the reflected object. Thus then those alone are the right thinkers who differentiate the cogniser, the cognition and the cognised in their respective characters,—(basing the differentiation) on the difference in the mind as enlivened by each of them severally.

Notes :—(1) "*By the subjective soul to its functions*"—'its'—Of the soul. The function of the soul is nothing more than its reflection in the mind.

Wherefore is this? (Reply :)

Sutra (24) :—Though variegated by innumerable impressions, it exists for another, because it operates by association.

Com :—The mind, though variegated by innumerable impressions, yet exists for another's purpose,—that is to say, for the experience (or enjoyment) and liberation of others, not for its own purpose, because it operates by association, like a house. The mind, operating as it does by association, can never exist for itself. For certainly, a mind operating for pleasure is not for its own pleasure ; nor is wisdom for its own wisdom ; on the other hand, both of these are for another's purpose. This "another" is the soul with a purpose—the purpose being experience and liberation, and not any and everything other than mind. If the Nihilist were to bring forward any object at random (as being the "other" for whose sake the mind operates), all such objects would be found to be operating by association and as such, existing for the sake of something else. The particular "another," the soul, just spoken of does not operate by association.

Note :—(1) *Mind for "pleasure &c."*—"Pleasure" here implies *experience*, and "wisdom" *liberation*.

With this aphorism, of Sankhyakarika XVII. संघातपरार्थत्वात &c.

Sutra (25):—**For the knower of the difference, (there is) cessation of all thought of the nature of self.**

Com :—As in the rainy season, from the sprouting forth of grass is inferred the existence of the seed, so in the same manner, when we find a certain person horripilating and shedding tears of inward pleasure, we infer the existence of its seed in the shape of some peculiar deed, partaking of the nature of Bliss, done in the past (and now bearing its fruit). For such a one the natural hankering after the nature of self is (continually) operating. The absence of such deeds leads to what is thus declared: "having renounced his own nature, by reason of some deficiency, there arises a liking for the sceptic view and aversion to the standard doctrine; during this state is a hankering after the nature of self, in this form: Who was I? How was I? What is this? How is this? Who shall I be? How shall I be? This hankering ceases for one who attains discrimination. Why? Because this is a curious modification of the mind; the soul however, in the absence of Ignorance, is pure, untainted by the properties of the mind. Therefore, for such an expert the hankering after the nature of self ceases.

Notes :—(1) "The sceptic view &c."—*i. e.*, The Nihilist's sceptic position—viz: "There is no super-physical result of actions because of the non-existence of any super-physical region." The standard doctrine is the one expounded here.

Sutra (26):—Then the mind is turned towards discrimination, and is bowed down by Isolation.

Com :—The mind, that was bowed down by objects and bent towards ignorance, now becomes otherwise—i. e., bowed down by isolation and bent towards discriminative knowledge.

Notes :—"*Now*"—when the mind has become conscious of the difference.

Sutra (27) :—In the intervals thereof, there are other cognitions, due to impressions.

Com :—In the intervals of the mind, being bent towards the discrimination of itself, flowing in the current of the discrimination of matter and spirit, there are other cognitions such as, "I exist," "This is mine," "I know" or "I do not know." Whence? From the fading seeds, the foregone impressions.

Notes : (1)—"*Bent towards discrimination of itself*"—i. e., of the mind from the sentient faculty; Vachaspati Misra explains "*Pratyaya*" as that which cognises—i. e., the mind.

(2)—"*Flowing*] *in the current &c.*"—This explains the preceding epithet—'bent towards the discrimination of itself.'

(3)—"*Foregone impressions*"—i.e., the fading impressions of the former waking state.

During the progress of isolation, when in the intervals the mind rests from meditation, it is beset with some worldly ideas, sprouting from the non-fading impressions of the former waking state. Such ideas are impediments and should be avoided.

Sutra (28):—The destruction of these should be as already described in the case of the distractions.

Com:—As the distractions, on the destruction of their sprouting faculty, cease to be capable of sprouting up, so in the same manner, the foregone impression having its sprouting faculty burnt up by the fire of wisdom, ceases to give birth to consciousness (or cognition). The impressions due to wisdom however depend upon the destruction of the operative capacity of the mind ; and therefore these are not considered here.

Notes : (1)—" ***As already described in the case of the distractions*** **"—in Sec II, 10-11.**

(2)—" ***Impressions due to wisdom*** **"—i.e., to Supreme Dispassion. As these would naturally fall off on the destruction of the capacity of mind, so the means of the extirpation of these are not mentioned.**

Sutra (29) :—To the disinterested in even *illumination or discriminative knowledge* (accrues) exclusive discriminative wisdom leading to the meditation called the "Cloud of Virtue."

Com :—When such a Brâhmaṇa loses all interest in illumination even—i. e., who desires nothing even from that, and becomes indifferent to it,—to him accrues exclusive discriminative wisdom; and thus the seed of metempsychosis being destroyed, no more cognitions are produced; and thus proceeds the meditation called the "Cloud of Virtue."

Notes :—(1) "*Non-aspiring &c.*"—One who has no desire for any of the fruits proceeding from "illumination" by which is meant " the light of knowledge" resulting from discriminative recognition of the twenty-six elements of the Sankhya system; this illumination is described in *Sutra* 49, sec. III,.

(2)—" ***Cloud of Virtue*** **"—i.e., the condition in which all Virtues are showered down.**

(3)—The meaning of the Sutra is: "When after this illumination, the Yogin works entirely without any attachment or desire, he reaches the state of supreme non-attachment wherein the light of the soul breaks out in full." (Dvivedi) The sense is that though the Yogin may not wish for any reward, still the reward comes.

Satra (30):—Thence the cessation of distractions and actions.

Com:—On the attainment thereof, the distractions, Ignorance and the rest, are destroyed from their very roots, the good and bad actions also are put a stop to; and on the cessation of distractions and actions, the wise one becomes liberated, while living. Wherefore? Because misconception is the sole cause of worldliness. For certainly no one has ever witnessed the birth of one whose misconception has been removed.

Notes: (1)—"*Thereof*"—i.e., of the meditation called "Cloud of Virtue."

(2)—"*From their roots*"—The roots being the several kinds of impressions.

(3)—"*Is liberated*"—Because the cause of birth, life and experience, is the karmic residua enlivened by actions, distractions and impressions. Of the *Vaiseshika Sutra—Vitarâgajanmâdarsanât* ("On account of the non perception of the birth of one free from attachment)."

"On the appearance of the (aforesaid) Cloud there results a complete cessation of all afflictions and all works; there is no longer any sense of affliction left in the mind of the Yogi; and he has neither any desire for work, nor any residua of former works left in his mind."—*Mitra.*

Sutra (31):—Then, in consequence of the infiniteness of the knowledge free from all coverings and impurities, the knowable becomes small.

Com:—The infinity of knowledge results from its being free from the obscurations of action and distraction. The faculty of knowledge, suppressed under the obscuring **Tamas**, is only occasionally uncovered and rendered operative by (*Rajas*) and then becomes capable of cognising. Under the circumstances, when it becomes clear of all impurities and obscurations, then results its infiniteness. And from the infiniteness of knowledge, the knowable becomes small—like the firefly in the sky. In this connection it is declared: "The blind man pierced the gems, the fingerless one joined them together, the neckless one wore it, and the tongueless one praised it."

Notes: (1)—"*In this connection it is declared &c.*—Says Vachaspati Misra: "It may be objected—'granted that the Cloud of Virtue is the cause of the cessation of actions and distractions together with their impressions; but why should not the Yogin be born again even when this cloud exists?' The reply is given by the quotation. (The sense of the reply being that) if the effect be produced even on the removal of the cause, then the piercing of gems by the blind and the other circumstances mentioned in the quotation would also be possible."

Vijnâna Bhikshu however explains the quotation as a peculiar assertion of the Bauddha who says that such an ominiscience as is above described, is as great an impossibility as the circumstances mentioned in the quotation.

Sutra (32) :—Thereupon follows the termination of the succession of the modifications of the Attributes, which have accomplished their end.

Com :—On the appearance of the Cloud of Virtue, end the successive modifications of the Attributes whose ends have been fulfilled. Because (Attributes), that have fulfilled experience and liberation, and whose succession has ended, dare not tarry a moment longer.

Note :—This aphorism meets the objection that, though actions and distractions would end, still the attributes, from their very mobile nature, would continue to undergo modifications and thus produce birth, experience &c. The sense of the reply is that the nature of the Attributes is such that when once their purpose (the experience and liberation of the soul) has been fulfilled, they cease to operate, with regard to that particular soul.—cf the concluding *Sânkhya Kârikâs*.

What is this succession? (Reply:)

Sutra (33):—The succession is the counterpart of the moment perceptible at the end of the modification.

Com:—The succession, consisting in the intervals of moments, is perceived by the end of modification. For the oldness of a new piece of cloth, at its end (destruction), does not follow without the consciousness of the successive moment (of its duration). This succession is seen to exist even with regard to eternal objects. The eternality is two-fold—the unchanging eternality, and the modifying eternality. Of these the unchanging eternality belongs to the Soul and the modifying eternality to the Attributes. That object is eternal the modifications whereof do not destroy its real form. And as the forms of both Soul and the Attributes are not destroyed, therefore both of them are eternal. With regard to the products of the Attributes—Buddhi and the rest—the succession, perceptible at the end of the modification, has its own end perceptible; whereas it has not its end perceptible in the case of the eternal objects, ; the Attributes themselves with regard to the unchanging eternal, the liberated souls, existing in their own form, the existence of the form is perceived in succession; and here too, the succession, having its end non-perceptible, is assumed through the *action of existence*,—the assumption being based up on "word."

Question:—"Of this Universe, existing in the Attributes by its existence and progress, is there an end to the succession or not?" Reply:—This indeed is unanswerable! Why? The question admitting of an absolute reply is such as 'Will all that is born, die?' (The reply is): "Oh! Yes." On the other hand, there is another question (not admitting of an absolute reply) such as "will every object that dies be born? The answer to this question must be a qualified one viz., the wise one whose desires have been destroyed and who has attained discrimination, will not be born ; others besides such a one, will be surely born. Similarly on being asked 'Is the human species the highest or not ?' the reply must be given in a qualified form : The human species is higher than the other animals, whereas it is not so in comparison with the Gods and the Rishis. The question "Has the universe an end or not ?" is unanswerable directly ; because (the reply must be ;) 'for the wise one (above mentioned), there is an end to the continuance of the universe,—not for any other.' For this reason, if the reply were based on any *one of the two*, i. e., if the reply were given directly—yes or no—without qualification, there would be a mistake. Hence the aforesaid question must be broken up (before being answered.)

Notes : (1)—" The word "*succession*" is explained in this aphorism to mean the following of one momont after another. The object is to say that the lapse of time is reckoned by the succession of one moment after another, though there is a break between them one totality is divided into many parts only for facility of reckening."—*Mitra.*

It has been declared that Isolation follows at the end of the succession of the capacity of the Attributes. This Isolation is now described :

Sutra (34) :—The repression of the Attributes, devoid of the soul's purpose, is the Isolation; or it is the sentient faculty abiding in itself.

Com :—The repression (or inverse resolution) of the Attributes of the nature of cause and effect, that have fulfilled experience and isolation, and are (hence) unable to serve any further purpose of the soul, is Isolation. The sentient faculty of the soul abiding in itself, i.e., disconnected from the attributes of Buddhi, is pure; and (such a sentient faculty) continuing for ever in that condition, constitutes Isolation.

THE END

4 444000 358239